T0311695

Cambridge Elements ≡

Elements in the Philosophy of Mind
edited by
Keith Frankish
The University of Sheffield

THE METAPHYSICS OF MIND

Janet Levin
University of Southern California

CAMBRIDGE
UNIVERSITY PRESS

CAMBRIDGE
UNIVERSITY PRESS

University Printing House, Cambridge CB2 8BS, United Kingdom

One Liberty Plaza, 20th Floor, New York, NY 10006, USA

477 Williamstown Road, Port Melbourne, VIC 3207, Australia

314–321, 3rd Floor, Plot 3, Splendor Forum, Jasola District Centre,
New Delhi – 110025, India

103 Penang Road, #05–06/07, Visioncrest Commercial, Singapore 238467

Cambridge University Press is part of the University of Cambridge.

It furthers the University's mission by disseminating knowledge in the pursuit of
education, learning, and research at the highest international levels of excellence.

www.cambridge.org
Information on this title: www.cambridge.org/9781108925075
DOI: 10.1017/9781108946803

First published 2022

A catalogue record for this publication is available from the British Library.

ISBN 978-1-108-92507-5 Paperback
ISSN 2633-9080 (online)
ISSN 2633-9072 (print)

The Metaphysics of Mind

Elements in the Philosophy of Mind

DOI: 10.1017/9781108946803
First published online: February 2022

Janet Levin
University of Southern California
Author for correspondence: Janet Levin, levin@usc.edu

Abstract: This Element presents and discusses the major contemporary theories of the nature of mind, including Dualism, Physicalism, Role Functionalism, Russellian Monism, Panpsychism, and Eliminativism. Its primary goal is to examine the strengths and weaknesses of the theories in question, including their prospects for explaining the special qualitative character of sensations and perceptual experiences; the special outer-directedness of beliefs, desires, and other intentional states; and – more generally – the place of the mind in the world of nature, and the relation between mental states and the behaviors that they (seem to) cause. It also discusses, briefly, some further questions about the metaphysics of mind, namely, whether groups of individuals, or entire communities, can possess mental states that cannot be reduced to the mental states of the individuals in those communities and whether the boundaries between mind and world are as sharp as they may seem.

Keywords: mind–body problem, Dualism, Physicalism, consciousness, belief

ISBNs: 9781108925075 (PB), 9781108946803 (OC)
ISSNs: 2633-9080 (online), 2633-9072 (print)

Contents

1 Introduction

It seems obvious that we humans have mental states such as thoughts, beliefs, desires, sensations, and emotions – or at least as obvious as that we have physical states such as height, weight, and hair color. It also seems obvious that changes in our physical states can cause changes in our mental states, and vice versa: touching a hot stove will (normally) cause us to feel pain, think that we've been careless, and want the pain to stop – which, in turn, will cause us to wince, or curse, or run to the freezer to get some ice. However, although these claims may seem obvious, they raise a number of questions that do not have obvious answers.

Some of these questions about mental states are *metaphysical* questions: What kinds of things are thoughts, desires, sensations, and emotions; what is their relation to the physical states of our bodies and brains; and how do changes in physical states produce changes in mental states, and vice versa? Another metaphysical question is whether nonhuman creatures can also have mental states, and if so, which creatures – for example, chimps, cats, octopuses, androids – and which types of states – for example, sensations, thoughts, hopes, fears?

There are also *epistemological* questions in this domain; among them are how we could know whether chimps, cats, octopuses, androids – and indeed humans other than ourselves – have mental states, and if so, whether those states are similar to our own. Indeed, there are questions about how we come to know about our *own* mental states and whether we could ever think that we think something, want something, or feel something – and be wrong. There are *moral* questions in this domain as well; among them are whether creatures that can think or feel should be treated differently from those that cannot and whether we are entitled to expect creatures that can think or feel to treat us in certain ways.

This Element focuses on the metaphysical questions. However, as will become clear, the answers to the metaphysical questions have implications for the others – and vice versa – and so these other questions cannot be ignored entirely in evaluating different theories about the nature (and extent) of mental states and their relation to the physical world. Thus, while these questions will not be the focus of attention, they cannot be completely ignored.

On the other hand, this Element does not aim to present every metaphysical theory of mind that has been proposed throughout the history of philosophy but focuses instead on five that – at least arguably – are taken most seriously in contemporary work on the subject. These are *Dualism, the (Mental–Physical) Type Identity Theory, Role Functionalism, Russellian Monism,* and *Eliminativism* (or Illusionism).

Dualism is the thesis that the mental and the physical are two distinct kinds of things, each independent of, and irreducible to, the other. Dualism has three major varieties: *Substance* (or *Cartesian*) *Dualism*, the thesis that physical and mental states are states of two distinct types of substances such as material substances that occupy space and are capable of motion and immaterial substances that exist outside of space; *Property Dualism*, the thesis that while there are no immaterial substances, there are certain sufficiently complex material substances (such as human brains) that have states or properties that are irreducibly mental; and *Panpsychism*, the thesis that all things, from atoms to humans to planets, have both physical and irreducibly mental states.

The *Type Identity Theory* is a species of *Physicalism*, the thesis that minds and mental states are nothing over and above bodies and physical states. Evaluations of Physicalism often include debates about whether there is *anything* in the world that is nonphysical, for example, immaterial gods, ghosts, or even numbers. The concern here is narrower, however, and focuses on whether (human) mental states, and all their properties, are physical. The Type Identity Theory is the claim that each type of mental state (e.g. the feeling of pain, the thought that today is Friday, the desire for chocolate) is identical with some type of physical state, presumably some state of the brain and central nervous system, for example, that pain is identical with a certain sort of C-fiber stimulation. Type Identity statements, therefore, can be true only if all (and only) instances of a particular type of mental state (e.g. pain) are instances of the same physical type (e.g. C-fiber stimulation).

There is another species of Physicalism, *Nonreductive Physicalism*, that does not require type identity, but only that each particular instance (or "token") of a type of mental state be identical with a token of some type of physical state or other. On this view, creatures with physical states very different from our own could nonetheless have the same mental states as we do, as long as we have certain other properties in common that are not irreducibly mental. Different Nonreductive Physicalist theories specify different properties to play this role, but the most common species of Nonreductive Physicalism is *Role Functionalism*.

Role Functionalism is the thesis that what makes something a mental state is not its internal constitution, but the role it plays, the function it has, in an individual's psychology. Role Functionalism too has a number of varieties. These arise from differences in which sorts of roles are viewed as definitive of mental states and which sources of information can be used to specify those roles. Common Sense (or Analytic) Functionalism requires that information be derived from our commonly held "platitudes" about the causal roles of mental states in the production of other mental states and behavior, while

Psychofunctionalism (or Empirical Functionalism) permits information from empirical psychology and neurophysiology to have a role in characterizing mental states, even if it is not commonly known.

All versions of Physicalism, in contrast to Dualism, are species of Monism, the thesis that there is just one fundamental type of thing in the world from which everything else is derived. There are other species of Monism, including *Idealism*, the thesis that the fundamental constituents of the world are minds and their perceptions, thoughts, and volitions, and *Neutral Monism*, the thesis that the fundamental constituents of the world are neither physical nor mental, but rather "neutral" properties from which both physical and mental states arise. Although there are different varieties of Neutral Monism, one of the most interesting for contemporary philosophers is Russellian Monism.

Russellian Monism derives from Bertrand Russell's (1927) view that the physical sciences describe only the structural or dispositional properties of the things that occur in nature and that these dispositions must be grounded in, or underlain by, intrinsic or categorical properties. In Russell's view, these categorical properties not only ground the dispositional states described by the physical sciences but also provide the basis of our conscious experiences.

Although Dualism and the various species of Monism may seem to exhaust the possibilities for a theory of minds and mental states, there is one further theory that warrants discussion: Eliminativism.

Eliminativism (or Illusionism) is the thesis that there are no such things as mental states and properties – or at least no states that possess certain essential features that we commonly assume sensations, perceptions, beliefs, or desires to have. Some Eliminativists direct their skepticism to sensations and perceptual experiences; others to beliefs and desires – and they do so for importantly different reasons.

This may seem to be a tidy categorization of the available theories of mind, but there is some debate about which views belong to which categories; is Nonreductive Physicalism really a species of Physicalism; is Neutral Monism genuinely neutral; is the Type Identity Theory just Eliminativism in disguise? Even more broadly, there is debate about the proper characterization of Physicalism itself.[1]

Moreover, one need not expect any one theory to provide the best account of all types of mental states; one can pick and choose among them, giving up unity for plausibility. For example, one can, and many do, endorse Role

---

[1] Should physical states be characterized as the states described by our *current* physical (and chemical and biological theories) or by the theories that will emerge at the end of scientific inquiry? See Hempel, 1969. This debate, however, does not affect this discussion of the metaphysics of mind.

Functionalism as a theory of thoughts, beliefs, and desires but prefer the Identity Thesis – or even Dualism – as an account of perceptual experiences and bodily sensations. Or one can adopt Eliminativism for beliefs and desires but endorse the Identity Theory (or Dualism or Functionalism) for sensations and perceptual experiences.

In the sections to follow, I will present these five theories of the nature of mental states and sketch their primary strengths and weaknesses. In doing so, I will pay special attention to how well they account for what seem to be the distinctive properties of states such as sensations and perceptual experiences, namely, their *qualitative (or phenomenal) character*, or, in Thomas Nagel's (1974) now-classic locution, *what it is like* for someone to be in those states. I will also focus on how well these theories capture what seem to be the distinctive properties of states such as thoughts, beliefs, and desires, namely, their capacity to *represent* – or *be about* – items in the world.

Here too, however, there is no tidy categorization; many philosophers argue that even though there are important differences between thinking and feeling, sensations and perceptual experiences can represent items in the world (or in one's body) in addition to having qualitative character, and some argue that thoughts can have specific qualitative characters in addition to representing items in the world. Indeed, some argue that sensations *must* be representational and thoughts *must* have a qualitative character.[2] These views are contentious, but if they are true, then the problems raised for sensations and perceptual experiences will extend to thoughts – and vice versa.

As will (or should) become clear, there is no knockdown argument for or against any of these theories, and they all have features, or implications, that may violate our commonsense, pre-theoretical views about what mental states are, what sorts of creatures can have them, and what their relation is to bodily states. This has prompted some (e.g. Schwitzgebel, 2014) to question whether it's rational to accept any of these theories – even while recognizing that one (or some combination) of them has to be true, since they exhaust the possibilities. In my estimation, this verdict is too pessimistic. Although I will try to give a fair account of the strengths and weaknesses of all the views in question, readers may weigh these strengths and weaknesses differently and judge that there are good (if not airtight) reasons to accept one or the other of these views.

---

[2] For a good example of the first, see Byrne (2001), and of the second, see Horgan and Tienson (2002).

However, in the final section, I will (briefly) present some further, recently articulated, questions about the relation between mental states and individual brains and bodies that arise for almost any theory of the metaphysics of mental states. These questions are puzzling and important, and they are just beginning to be discussed. Thus, even for those who clearly prefer one (or some combination) of the theories discussed in these sections, there is still a lot of work to be done to determine the relation of mental to physical states and the place of the mind in the natural world.

2 Dualism

There are many varieties of Dualism – the thesis that mental and physical states are distinct from and irreducible to one another – but all hold that in a world containing nothing but physical objects, events, and properties, there would be no creatures with thoughts, sensations, volitions, or any other sort of mental states. For that, the world must include something more.

But what is this "something more"; which creatures possess it; and what is the relation between whatever it is and the world of physical objects? These are questions that the different varieties of Dualism answer in different ways.

According to Substance Dualism, for there to be creatures with mental, as well as physical, states and processes, the world must include immaterial substances – minds (or equivalently, souls) that can think, perceive, and will – in addition to the bodies that take up space, have the capacity to move, and can be perceived by the senses. Although this was the dominant view in the ancient and medieval world, in contemporary discussions, it is associated primarily with Rene Descartes (and often called Cartesian Dualism) – for two reasons. One is that Descartes was among the first to characterize the mind as we now conceive it, namely, as the locus of conscious mental activities exclusively (i.e. thinking, feeling, and willing), rather than those activities plus others distinctive to living things, such as locomotion and respiration. Another is that Descartes's most influential argument for the distinction between mind and body, which he presents in Meditation Six of his *Meditations on First Philosophy* (1641/1984), provides the template for the most influential contemporary arguments for Dualism, and the responses to this argument by Descartes's own interlocutors provide the template for the most influential responses to those contemporary arguments.

This argument, in brief, is:

1. I can clearly and distinctly understand myself to exist apart from my body.
2. If I can clearly and distinctly understand x to exist apart from y, then it is possible for x to exist apart from y.

3. If it is possible for x to exist apart from y, then x is not the same thing as y.

> THEREFORE
>
> I am not the same thing as my body.[3]

Many find the conclusion of this argument attractive since it opens up the possibility that one's mind, and thus one's self, could be immortal – or at least continue to exist for some time after the destruction of one's body. The premises of this argument, however, need explication – and defense.

For Descartes, to have a clear and distinct understanding of something is to have a conception of it that reveals its nature or essence, that is, the properties it must possess in order to exist – and we attain clear and distinct understanding by considering our ordinary idea of something and thinking carefully about which properties it can lose and which it must retain to remain that very same thing. Descartes defends premise 1 by arguing that he has a clear and distinct conception of himself as (essentially) something that thinks (i.e. as the locus of conscious mental activity) and a clear and distinct conception of his body as (essentially) something that occupies space – and that it is perfectly coherent to think of things that occupy space as lacking conscious mental activity, and vice versa.[4]

This premise may seem plausible, at least initially. But some of Descartes's contemporaries, most famously Pierre Gassendi, argued that Descartes's reports of his own clear and distinct conceptions may just be wrong. As Gassendi puts it in his Objections to *Descartes's Meditations* (1641/1984), Descartes's supposed understanding of himself as an immaterial substance may really be a conception of himself as "a wind, or rather a very thin vapour ... diffused through the parts of the body and giving them life."[5] Gassendi's question, in short, is whether we can be wrong about what the contents of our clear and distinct conceptions *are* – and as will become clear, this worry informs contemporary discussions of the metaphysics of mind as well.

---

[3] This argument is extracted from the following passage:

> First, I know that everything which I clearly and distinctly understand is capable of being created by God so as to correspond exactly with my understanding of it. Hence the fact that I can clearly and distinctly understand one thing apart from the other is enough to make me certain that the two things are distinct, since they are capable of being separated, at least by God ... [Now] on the one hand I have a clear and distinct idea of myself, insofar as I am simply a thinking, non-extended thing; and on the other hand I have a distinct idea of body, insofar as this is simply an extended, non-thinking thing. And accordingly, it is certain that I am really distinct from my body, and can exist without it. Descartes (1641/1984, p. 53).

[4] However, there are versions of Substance Dualism in which immaterial substances can have spatial location. See Hart (1988) and Latham (2001).

[5] See Gassendi (1640/1984), p. 180. The argument gets quite heated – on both sides: see Descartes's Reply to Fifth Set of Objections 1641/1984): 241-267.

Premise 2 may also seem dubious, especially since Descartes defends it by appealing to the existence and nondeceptiveness of God (which he claims to have proven in, respectively, in his *Third* and *Fourth Meditation*). If God exists and is truly nondeceptive, Descartes argues, then we must possess some sort of faculty that, if used correctly, will get us to the truth. And what better candidate could there be for such a faculty than clear and distinct understanding!

Here too, however, Descartes's contemporaries, most famously Antoine Arnauld, raised questions about the connection between clear and distinct understanding and possibility. In his Objections to *Descartes's Meditations* (1641/1984), Arnauld argues that there is an obvious counterexample to premise 2, namely, that someone can clearly and distinctly understand that a triangle is right-angled, without needing to understand that it obeys the Pythagorean theorem, and thus, it would follow that there can be "a right-angled triangle with the square on its hypotenuse not equal to (the sum of) the squares on the other sides" (1641/1984, p. 182) – which is obviously impossible.

Descartes's response to this objection is to argue that to have a clear and distinct understanding of something, one needs to have a sufficiently "complete" conception of it to guarantee its existence. And when one has a sufficiently complete conception of what it is to be a right triangle *and* what it is to be a figure that obeys the Pythagorean theorem, one will be able, at least in principle, to see that if one exists, so must the other – and so this case is no counterexample to premise 2.

However, even if Descartes's response to Arnauld is convincing, contemporary thinkers may be reluctant to embrace a principle that makes the link between what we can conceive and what is possible dependent on the existence and nondeceptiveness of God. But even if they are skeptical of Descartes's defense of this premise, many contemporary thinkers agree that if there is any way we understand the world that can provide reliable evidence for claims about what is possible – and thus about the nature or essence of things – it will be something like Descartes's clear and distinct understanding. In achieving this sort of understanding, we've tried our best and thereby have the best possible evidence for such claims!

So if Substance (Cartesian) Dualism were true, it would support the firm and widespread intuition that the distinctive features of our conscious mental states are so radically different from any physical states, events, or properties – either macroscopic or microscopic – that they could not be (or be explained by) anything exclusively physical. This has come to be known as the "hard problem of consciousness" (Chalmers, 1995). There are many examples of this intuition throughout the history of Western philosophy, for example, Leibniz's argument that no physical substance whose workings can be explained by mechanistic principles could possibly think or perceive:

> If we imagine that there is a machine whose structure makes it think, sense, and have perceptions, we could conceive it enlarged, keeping the same proportions, so that we could enter into it, as one enters a mill. Assuming that, when inspecting its interior, we will find only parts that push one another, and we will never find anything to explain a perception
>
> (1714/1991, section 17).

Another well-known example is T.H. Huxley's skepticism about the possibility of a neurophysiological explanation of conscious experience:

> How it is that anything as remarkable as a state of consciousness comes about as a result of irritating nerve tissue, is just as unaccountable as the appearance of the Djin, where Aladdin rubbed his lamp in the story (1875).

There are many other examples in between – and since – among them is McGinn, who asks: "How is it possible for mental states to depend upon brain states? How can technicolour experience arise from soggy grey matter?" (1989, p. 349).

However, although Substance Dualism has its attractions, it also has serious problems. First, it introduces a new type of substance, immaterial minds, into the world and thereby raises questions about when these substances get created, whether (and if so, how and why) they may be destroyed, and how many (and which sorts) of one's mental states (ideas) they may retain after the death of the body. More generally, one may wonder whether there are more parsimonious ways to explain how humans think, feel, and act; can this be done without appeal to immaterial minds? Moreover, if minds and bodies are distinct substances, it is hard to explain the seeming unity of mind and body that we experience in ordinary human life when our sensations and beliefs seem immediately and inextricably linked to what is going on in our bodies. Descartes himself recognizes the difficulty, later in Meditation Six of his *Meditations on First Philosophy* (1641/1984), where he acknowledges that:

> Nature . . . teaches me, by these sensations of pain, hunger, thirst, and so on, that I am not merely present in my body as a sailor is present in a ship, but that I am very closely joined and, as it were, intermingled with it, so that I and the body form a unit. If this were not so, I, who am nothing but a thinking thing, would not feel pain when the body was hurt, but would perceive the damage purely by the intellect, just as a sailor perceives by sight if anything in his ship is broken.

This intermingling is beneficial, Descartes suggests, because having sensations of pain and pleasure is an effective way of getting information about the helpful and harmful conditions in our environment. But it is hard to take these remarks about intermingling literally, since it is hard to understand how an immaterial substance that does not occupy space could "intermingle" with a body that does. Therefore, most theorists understand Descartes to be claiming that what unifies the mind and body of an individual is the existence of a unique, direct *causal connection* between that individual's physical and mental states: I put my hand near the burner on the stove, which causes me to feel heat and believe that moving closer would be painful, which, in turn, causes me to move my hand away. Such directness and (relative) immediacy occurs when, and only when, *my* bodily states produce *my* mental states (and vice versa) – and this is enough to explain the seeming unity of my mind with my body that I experience when I interact with the world.[6]

However, it is also difficult for a Substance Dualist to explain just how mind–body causation works. In *The Passions of the Soul*, Descartes proposes that "There is a little gland in the brain where the soul exercises its functions more particularly than in the other parts of the body" (1649/1984, section 31); that is, the pineal gland, which, as he puts it (1649/1984, section 32), serves as a kind of "funnel" by which neural activity in one's brain can have effects on the mind (soul) that correspond with those bodily (neural) activities. Causation also occurs in the other direction: the mind (soul) can act, via the pineal gland, to produce changes in one's brain that in turn have various differential effects on the body, such as moving its limbs.

Descartes's proposal, however, does not provide much insight into *how* this happens; how it is that neural activity can produce changes in an immaterial substance; and – even more puzzling – how an immaterial substance can produce changes in a body, especially given phenomena such as the conservation of energy and the principle that every physical event has a (sufficient) physical cause. This worry was expressed particularly forcefully by one of Descartes's contemporaries, Princess Elisabeth of Bohemia, who in a long correspondence with Descartes (1643–1647) asks how "the soul of a human being [which] is only a *thinking* substance ... can ... affect the bodily spirits, in order to bring about voluntary actions," given that causation requires "*contact* between the two things, [which in turn] requires that the causally active thing be extended" (1643/2017, p. 1).

---

[6] Some scholars, however, argue that Descartes regards humans as a third kind of substance and that they should be regarded as "trialists" rather than dualists. Among others, see Hoffman (1986).

Descartes (1643/2017, p. 3) responds by suggesting that the problem arises because we have confused the notion of "the soul's power to act on bodies with the body's power to act on other bodies" – and that soul–body causation is a different sort of process that requires neither contact nor energy transmission. However, he never says just what this process is, but only that something like this *has* to occur, since he's proven that minds (souls) are distinct from bodies, and we know that there is causal interaction between them!

Clearly, one way to resolve this dilemma without abandoning Dualism is to give up the claim that there is causal interaction between mental and physical states. Some of Descartes's (near) contemporaries do just this and argue that although it may seem that the mind has an effect on the body (and vice versa), this is an illusion. One view, Parallelism, contends that mental and physical events occur in perfect parallel and do not interact at all – due to God's having set things up this way and then letting things in each domain unfold through time in preestablished harmony. Another view, Occasionalism (associated primarily with Malebranche), contends that when it seems as though a physical event in my body is causing something to go on in my mind, what is *really* happening is that God is taking the occurrence of that physical event to be an occasion for producing some mental state in me.

These alternatives will not be pursued further, since their problems are no doubt salient. But it is important to recognize that at least some Dualists at the time were willing, in one way or another, to abandon the claim that there is causal interaction between mental and physical states. As will become clear, the worries expressed in this seventeenth-century dialectic, especially about how mental states (as understood by Descartes) could cause bodily states, remain major worries for Dualism even today.

A further question for Substance Dualism concerns just which physical creatures possess immaterial minds. Descartes (1637/1984) himself argues that humans are the only creatures with minds as well as bodies, on the grounds that – as he argues in the *Discourse on Method* (and other places) – humans are the only (mortal) creatures capable of thought and rationality. We know this, he argues, because only humans can use language and behave appropriately in a wide range of situations, and it is these capacities that, as Descartes puts it, distinguish "man from beast," and also human from mere machine. Admittedly, there has long been a dispute about whether all nonhuman animals lack the linguistic capacities and response flexibility that Descartes requires for having a mind, and there is increasing debate about whether machines could someday possess them. But it is hard, nonetheless, to settle on criteria for what it takes to make the cut.

In addition, if minds are immaterial substances that can be directly perceived only by the individuals who possess them, it is difficult to explain how we can know that someone else is in pain, is happy about getting promoted, or believes that the coffee is too hot. It may seem as if we can attain this knowledge by analogy with our own case, that is, by projecting the feelings and beliefs *we* have in certain situations onto others we observe to be in similar circumstances, but – as many have argued in response to this suggestion – successful "arguments from analogy" usually proceed from a base of more than one case.

Some of these problems, however, are avoided by another version of Dualism, Property Dualism, which maintains that while there are no immaterial substances in the world, there are certain physical substances – among them the brains and central nervous systems of sufficiently complex creatures – that possess not only physical properties such as shape, mass, color, and so on but also irreducible mental properties. These include the qualitative (or phenomenal) properties of sensations and perceptual experiences – *what it's like* to be in pain or experience red – and also the special characteristics of beliefs, thoughts, and volitions that determine what, in the world outside the mind, they are *about* or *represent*.

Property Dualism, the view preferred by most contemporary Dualists, can thereby support the intuition that mental and physical states are radically different without having to introduce immaterial substances into the world and explain how they "intermingle" with their associated bodies. To be sure, Property Dualism introduces two distinct kinds of properties into the world, but as some Dualists argue, there is an explanation for why some physically complex systems possess both mental and physical properties.

For example, Huxley, the well-known expositor and defender of Darwinism (quoted previously), proposes that the existence of creatures with enough neurophysiological complexity to have conscious mental states is due to natural selection (although he also argues, in response to Descartes's contention that conscious states are exclusive to humans, that certain nonhuman animals are enough like us neurophysiologically to be likely to possess them as well). However, Huxley suggests, although conscious states arise from "molecular changes in the brain," they "would appear to be related to the mechanism of their body simply as a collateral product of its working and to be as completely without power of modifying that working as the steam whistle which accompanies the work of a locomotive engine is without influence on its machinery" (2002, p. 29).

That is, just as the engine simultaneously produces the opening and closing of the valves and the whistling noise, various kinds of neural activity in a sufficiently complex subject simultaneously produce some further neural state in that subject (perhaps stimulation of the motor neurons) and *also* the feeling of wanting or willing to move in certain ways. However, Huxley continues, "[this] volition . . . [would be] an emotion indicative of physical changes, not a cause of such changes"[7] (1875/2002, p. 29).

On this view (shared by many Property Dualists), Property Dualism is consistent with the thesis that every physical event has a sufficient physical cause and also with the principle of the conservation of energy, since physical changes cause mental changes in addition to, rather than instead of, further physical changes. Nonetheless, Property Dualism faces the converse question about mental–physical causation. It seems obvious that changes in one's mental states can cause changes in one's physical states, as well as the other way around: I feel pain in my hand, say "ouch," and move it away from the burner; I want some ice and believe there is some in the freezer, and so I walk over to the freezer and open the door. A view that, like Huxley's, makes mental states causally powerless, or epiphenomenal, must regard these seemingly obvious truths as illusions – and this seems contrary to our experience of what goes on when we act.

There is another variety of Property Dualism that provides a different way to think about minds and their place in nature. This is Panpsychism, the thesis that all the elementary particles in the universe possess *both* physical *and* conscious mental properties.[8] Most versions of both Substance and Property Dualism hold that conscious mental states first make their appearance in humans (and perhaps some nonhuman animals), and this raises the question of why, and how, this occurs. Descartes appeals to God to explain why conscious mental states occur (in humans), and others (e.g. Huxley) suggest that their occurrence, in humans and certain other animals, is the (by-) product of evolution.

But for those who find these explanations arbitrary, Panpsychism maintains that mental properties are among the fundamental features of the world; they, just like physical properties, have been there all along. Moreover, if mental properties essentially occur along with physical properties even at the basic physical level, then they are essential components of the causes of all events that occur in the world, including human behavior – and thus, it should be no more mysterious that the states we call "pain" or "belief" could cause me to move my hand than that hitting a billiard ball with a cue stick could cause it to

---

[7] There are some passages, however, that suggest that Huxley himself is a Substance Dualist.

[8] See Nagel (1979) for a well-known contemporary statement of the view. Some who call themselves Panpsychists, however, are Monists and hold that conscious mental (i.e. phenomenal) properties are the only fundamental properties of the universe, which, when combined in certain ways, yield full-fledged conscious experiences. See Goff (2017) for a good example of this view.

move.[9] These are primary attractions of Panpsychism, and it has been embraced by a number of philosophers since the pre-Socratics and is undergoing somewhat of a revival now.[10]

Nonetheless, Panpsychism, like all forms of Dualism, proposes that there are two distinct kinds of properties in the world – mental and physical – and this may seem extravagant, even if some sort of conscious mental properties are among the fundamental features of the world. Moreover, Panpsychism faces what is known as the combination problem – or better the combination problems – since it must explain how microscopic glimmers of consciousness combine to produce the familiar sensations and perceptual experiences of our everyday mental lives and also how microscopic subjects with glimmers of consciousness combine to produce macroscopic subjects like ourselves.[11] Finally, many find it implausible that the elementary particles of physics are capable of having any degree of consciousness whatsoever.

To address this final worry, many contemporary Panpsychists endorse a more attenuated variation of the view, sometimes called Pan*proto*psychism, which maintains that although elementary particles have properties that are nonphysical, they do not exhibit consciousness themselves, and those properties do not contribute to genuine conscious experiences unless combined together in systems that are sufficiently complex (such as bodies with brains). This view, unlike Panpsychism, need not attribute even the glimmerings of conscious experience to elementary particles. However, it needs to say something about what these "proto" nonphysical properties are – and also (as with Panpsychism) to explain how they combine to produce full-fledged conscious states such as the feeling of pain or the experience of green.

Clearly, all varieties of Dualism have problems. Nonetheless, there are powerful arguments against all varieties of its most widely held rival, Physicalism, which maintains that there is only *one* kind of thing in the world, the physical. On this view, mental states and properties are nothing over and above physical states and properties; that is, in a world that contains all the physical entities in our world – but nothing else – there will be creatures with thoughts, sensations, and volitions as well. Like Dualism, however, there are different versions of Physicalism, each with its own strengths and weaknesses. One of the best-known varieties of Physicalism, the *Type Identity Theory*, is the topic of the following section.

---

[9] On the other hand, given the causal closure of the physical, one might contend that Panpsychism would make *all* causation mysterious!

[10] See Goff, Seager, and Hermanson (2017) for further details about the view and its advocates.

[11] See Brüntrup and Jaskolla (2016) and Seager (2020), section IV, for essays that present solutions to these problems – and objections to those solutions.

3 The Type Identity Theory

Unlike Dualism, Physicalism (often called "Materialism") maintains that the mental is nothing over and above the physical. All that is required for creatures to have sensations, thoughts, desires, emotions, or any other mental states is for there to be certain physical states and processes occurring in their brains and bodies (and perhaps in the world around them).

Although Physicalism had at least some adherents in both the Classical and Modern periods,[12] Dualism was the dominant view among Western philosophers until the middle of the twentieth century. Since then, however, many Western philosophers have endorsed some variety of Physicalism – either the Type Identity Theory or various forms of Nonreductive Physicalism, especially Role Functionalism – and differ only as to which provides the most plausible account of mental states.

This section focuses on the (contemporary) Type Identity Theory, first articulated by Place (1956/2002), Feigl (1958/2002), and Smart (1959/2002), namely, that for each type of mental state or process M, there is a type of brain state or process B such that M is identical with B (e.g. *pain* is the *stimulation of C-fibers*).[13] Since these claims are property identities, they entail that every instance of an M is a B, and vice versa. This view is more demanding than the (so-called) Token Identity Theory, which requires only that every token (instance) of a mental state be identical with a token of some physical state or other. However, if mental types cannot be identified with physical types, then Token Identity theorists who are Physicalists must hold either that there is another property shared by all mental states of a certain type that is not irreducibly mental – or that there are no mental types at all. The first alternative is endorsed by Nonreductive Physicalists; the second by Eliminativists. Both will be discussed in subsequent sections.

Early Type Identity theorists such as Place, Feigl, and Smart were particularly concerned to show that sensations and perceptual experiences, states with qualitative character or "feel," could be identical with types of brain processes, and this will also be the focus here. They recognized that the science of the time was far from establishing even a correlation between individuals' introspective reports of what they are feeling or thinking at some time and third-person

---

[12] Leucippus (fifth century BCE) and his student Democritus – and later Epicurus (341–270 BCE) and Lucretius (d.c. 50 BCE) – all contend that everything that exists in the world can be explained as configurations of, and interactions among, atoms in the void. In the Modern period, Descartes's contemporary Hobbes (1588–1679) and later La Mettrie (1709–1751) articulate physicalistic theories of mental states.

[13] Granted, the neural correlate of pain is more complicated than C-fiber stimulation, but "C-fiber stimulation" has become a stand-in in the philosophical literature for whatever the relevant state turns out to be.

reports (via instruments such as brain scans) of what is going on in their brains and bodies.[14] Their goal was to show, against intuitions (and arguments) to the contrary, that mental state–brain state identities are *possible* and that there are no logical or conceptual reasons to think that they could not be true. If these identities are possible and if there are in fact correlations between subjects' introspective reports and the results of simultaneous brain scans, then Type Identity theorists could argue that the simplest and most economical explanation of these correlations – and the one that avoids the other difficulties of Dualism – is that they are reporting on the same things.

But *is* the Identity Theory logically possible?[15] Many of the early objections to the theory appeal to what seem to be violations of Leibniz's Law (i.e. if $A = B$, then A and B must have all the same properties). For example, experiences are accessible only to the individuals who have them, while brain processes are publicly observable; experiences do not occur in physical space, while brain processes do. The Type Identity theorists' response to these objections is to argue that they beg the question: assuming, illicitly, that experiences are not physical processes.

A related class of objections maintain that we can *believe* that we are having some sensation without believing that there is anything going on in our brains (and vice versa) or that we can *conceive or imagine* that we are having some sensation in the absence of any brain activity (and vice versa). The Type Identity theorists' response to these objections is to argue that they arise from the assumption that if mental–physical identity statements are true, then they should be knowable a priori, that is, solely by reason and reflection, without need for empirical investigation.

However, the response continues; this assumption is false; there are many statements of this form that we believe to be true yet can be known only a posteriori, only by observations of the world as it happens to be.[16] These include familiar scientific identity statements such as "lightning is electrical

---

[14] Indeed, this remains a problem even now, since establishing such correlations requires trustworthy methods for measuring similarities and differences among the relevant neural states of a subject (and determining which are relevant). It also requires a standard vocabulary for producing introspective reports of what the subject is experiencing at that time; this is difficult enough for straightforward reports of degrees of pain and harder still for nonstandard states such as synaesthesia and psychedelic experiences.

[15] Although Smart's presentation of the Identity Thesis is not the earliest, it will be the focus here, since it clearly states the thesis, the objections to it, and the possible responses to those objections.

[16] This way of putting things is somewhat anachronistic, since Smart proposes that these identity statements (like all "theoretical" identity statements) are *contingent*, rather than necessary, but knowable only a posteriori. But it is the a posteriority of these theses that is the target of the objections and the responses to them.

discharge," "heat is mean kinetic energy," and "water is H_2O." So if there is no logical reason to doubt such scientific identity statements, there is no logical reason to doubt statements such as "pain is the stimulation of C-fibers" or (Smart's example) "the experience of a yellow-orange afterimage is brain process B," even if they seem dubious or outright false.

Although this analogy between mental state–brain state identity statements and other scientific identity statements may seem natural – and reasonable – the early Type Identity theorists faced a serious challenge to it, known as the "Distinct Property Objection." This (remarkably persistent) objection derives from Frege's (1892) semantic principle that the only way that a posteriori identity statements of the form $A = B$ can be true is for both A and B to denote their common referent R by being conceptually connected[17] to descriptions that pick out distinct properties of that referent, properties whose existence ensures the truth, respectively, of "R is A" and "R is B."[18]

This principle is satisfied by scientific identity statements such as "water is H_2O": "water" means (or is commonly associated with) "the colorless odorless liquid that comes out of our faucets" – and this description is uniquely satisfied by the stuff in the world that does just that – while "H_2O" means (or is commonly associated with) "the compound of two hydrogen atoms and one oxygen atom" – and this description is uniquely satisfied by the stuff in the world that is composed of just *that*. And if, in fact, it turns out that the colorless odorless stuff that comes out of our faucets is composed of hydrogen and oxygen atoms, then we have an explanation of how it is that "water is H_2O," though a posteriori, can be true. Similar explanations are available, moreover, for other scientific identity statements, such as "lightning is electrical discharge" and "heat is mean kinetic energy."

However, the objection continues; this principle cannot be satisfied by mental–physical identity statements: the only sorts of properties of some brain process B that could be uniquely picked out by descriptions commonly associated with "pain" or "the experience of a yellow-orange afterimage" and which insure the truth of "B is a pain" or "B is an experience of a yellow-orange afterimage" are *irreducibly qualitative* properties (e.g. feeling a certain distinctive way or being qualitatively yellowish-orange). But if this is so, then a sensation can be identical with a brain state only if that brain state possesses an irreducibly qualitative property in addition to a neural property such as

---

[17] This requires either that the term be equivalent in meaning to the description in question or that the description "fix the reference" of the term by being commonly understood to express a property that the referent uniquely, albeit contingently, possesses.

[18] In Smart's (1959) article, this appears as Objection 3 and is attributed to Max Black.

C-fiber stimulation – and this is incompatible with a purely physicalistic theory of mental states.[19]

Some contemporary Physicalists challenge the Fregean principle that underlies the Distinct Property Objection, and this may be the most promising way to put it to rest.[20] The early Type Identity theorists, however, took the objection seriously and proposed a solution to it, namely, to argue that mental state terms such as "pain" and "the experience of a yellow-orange afterimage" can be translated, preserving meaning, into "topic-neutral" descriptions, that is, descriptions that can be satisfied by *either* mental *or* physical states, processes, or events. If this is so, then there are properties by which mental state terms can denote brain states that are distinct from physical properties such as C-fiber stimulation yet are not irreducibly mental.

Smart was the first to propose this solution, suggesting that (e.g.) "I see a yellowish-orange afterimage" can be translated into "There is something going on [in me] which is like what goes on when I have my eyes open, am awake, and there is an [unripe] orange illuminated in good light in front of me." This description picks out a relational property that is "logically distinct" from any physical (or mental) property, and – if there really is a meaning equivalence between mental and topic-neutral terms – a state's having that topic-neutral property will indeed entail its being a mental state of the relevant sort.

Topic-neutral descriptions of this kind, however, were widely regarded as unsatisfactory, since they are not sufficiently specific to serve as (anything close to) translations of our ordinary mental state terms. After all, many different sensations and perceptions can be *like* what goes on in me when I'm looking at an unripe orange, in some way or another: I could be having an afterimage of a banana or a perception of a lime or a faded football. One needs to say more about the *way* in which my having an experience is like what goes on when I'm seeing an unripe orange, and – as many have argued – it's unclear that the relevant sort of resemblance can be specified in topic-neutral terms.

Other Type Identity theorists have attempted, with greater success, to provide topic-neutral equivalents of our ordinary mental state vocabulary. One well-known attempt is David Armstrong's (1981) suggestion that mental states of various types can be characterized in terms of their "aptness" to *cause* certain sorts of behavior or to be *caused by* certain environmental conditions, but he presents it as merely suggestive. The most developed, and best-regarded, account of this sort is David Lewis's (1972) proposal that topic-neutral translations of our mental state terms can be extracted from our "common sense

---

[19] See White (2007) for more recent versions of this argument and Block (2007) and Levin (2020) for a response.

[20] See, among others, Loar (1997). This response will be discussed further in Section 5.

theory" of the mind, which attempts to define mental states "all at once" by specifying (what we commonly believe to be) their causal interactions with environmental stimulations, behavior, and one another – as well as the similarities and differences and genus–species relations among them. Here is an (overly simplified) example, focusing on the state of pain:

> *Pain* is the state that tends to be caused by bodily injury, to produce the belief that something is wrong with the body and the desire to be out of that state, to produce anxiety, and, in the absence of any stronger, conflicting desires, to cause wincing or moaning.

Since this statement characterizes mental states solely in terms of the way they interact to produce behavior in response to various environmental conditions and the similarity relations among them, it is *topic-neutral* and can therefore be satisfied by either physical or irreducibly mental states and processes. Moreover, because these descriptions are extracted from our commonsense (or "folk") theory of mind, they can be regarded as explicating the meaning, or close enough, of our mental state terms and thus can be topic-neutral *translations* of those mental state terms. Therefore, if there are types of neural states in human beings that do in fact interact in ways that (uniquely) satisfy those descriptions, they will be identical with the sensations, beliefs, desires, and emotions that we attribute to ourselves and others – even if we cannot know this a priori.

Nonetheless, even if this is the most promising way to provide topic-neutral translations (or near enough) of our mental state terms, it may not be good enough: questions remain about whether these causal-relational characterizations can capture all the distinctive features of mental states, especially sensations and perceptions such as feeling pain or experiencing a yellow-orange afterimage. If not, there remains an important objection to the Type Identity Theory.

Similar questions are raised by some more recent arguments directed against any version of Physicalism, among them Saul Kripke's Modal Argument, David Chalmers's Zombie Argument, Thomas Nagel's Bat Argument, and Frank Jackson's Knowledge Argument. Because of the expanded scope of these arguments, further discussion of these questions will be postponed until Section 5. Now, however, it is time to address a different sort of objection to the Type Identity Theory, one that has been raised by many Physicalists themselves, namely, that its scope is too narrow and that it fails to capture psychological similarities between humans and other creatures who may be physically unlike us but seem, on other grounds, to have just the same mental states as we have.

Consider once again (the fragment of) Lewis's topic-neutral "commonsense" theory of pain:

> *Pain* is the state that tends to be caused by bodily injury, to produce the belief that something is wrong with the body and the desire to be out of that state, to produce anxiety, and, in the absence of any stronger, conflicting desires, to cause wincing or moaning.

This description, Lewis argues – along with the others that can be extracted from our commonsense theory – may well be (uniquely) satisfied by certain types of neural states and processes. And if so, as he argues, we would have grounds for believing that pain is identical with C-fiber stimulation – and so on for the other neural states uniquely specified by other clauses of our common sense theory. But this means that only creatures who share our neural states could have the same mental states that we have – and this seems too restrictive, or, as Ned Block (1980) puts it, too "chauvinistic."

After all, suppose there are creatures with internal states that are produced by environmental stimulations and interact with one another to produce behavior in just the way that ours do – but are physically quite different from our own. Think of the internal states of nonhuman animals such as octopuses, (hypothetical), silicon-based life forms on another planet, or androids built of titanium and electronic circuitry familiar from science fiction. According to the Type Identity Theory, these creatures could not have the same mental states as we do, even though their internal states interact to produce behavior in just the same ways as ours. And thus, not only could the human chauvinism of the Identity Thesis lead to discrimination against nonhuman life forms, but it would also narrow the explanatory scope of our psychological theories.

One response to this worry is to identify mental states with a *disjunction* of physical properties, for example, to suggest that pain is identical with *either* C-fiber stimulation *or* the relevant type of silicon-based state *or* the relevant type of electronic circuitry. But even this liberalized view could be too chauvinistic, since it would exclude creatures without those types of internal states from sharing our mental states, no matter how similar their behavior and its internal causes were to our own.

Another response to the worry about chauvinism is to identify mental states with coarser-grained neural states that may be possessed by humans, nonhuman animals, and perhaps other biological creatures.[21] But even if this suggestion

---

[21] See Polger and Shapiro (2018) for an argument that this coarse-grained individuation can include many creatures other than humans as capable of being in the same mental states and Bechtel and Mundale (1999) for an argument that neurophysiologists themselves use such coarser-grained characterizations.

bears fruit, it would rule out the possibility that nonbiological creatures such as androids could have mental states like our own.

There is yet another type of response to this problem, however, that many Physicalists endorse, namely, to identify mental states not with the types (or disjunction of types) of physical states that occupy a certain role in an individual's psychology but with those roles themselves, for example, to identify being in pain with the (higher-level) relational property of *being in some internal state or other* that plays the "pain role" in the psychological theory that holds of humans, octopuses, extraterrestrials, and androids. This theory, *Role Functionalism* (or the *Functional State Identity Theory*) gets further support from an analogy with computers: one can run the same computer program on different hardware systems – but the computational processes that the program directs will be relevantly the same. The strengths and weaknesses of Role Functionalism will be the focus of the following section.

4 Role Functionalism

Role Functionalism (or the Functional State Identity Theory) is the thesis that a type of mental state is not to be identified with a type of neural state or even a disjunction of different types of physical states, but rather with the (higher-level) property of *being in some internal state or other* that plays a certain role, or functions in a certain way, in a cognitive system.[22] Mental states themselves are to be identified with those higher-level causal-relational properties, whereas the lower-level states that play those roles are said to *realize* those states. And if different types of lower-level states can play those roles in different creatures, then those states are said to be *multiply realized*.

This is a different way of thinking about what it is to be a thinking, feeling individual, but it has historical precedents, among them Aristotle's theory of the soul (350 BCE), which considers the (human) soul as the set of capacities that enable the species *human* to fulfill the function or purpose that defines it as the kind of thing it is, namely, a *rational animal*. Another ancestor of Role Functionalism is Hobbes's (1651/2014, section 5) account of reasoning as a kind of computation that proceeds by mechanistic principles, which – along with imagining, sensing, and deliberating about action – can be performed by systems of various physical types.

Role Functionalism can also be viewed as a natural extension of Philosophical (as opposed to scientific) Behaviorism, a view of mental states introduced and defended by Norman Malcolm (1968), Gilbert Ryle (1949), and, arguably, Ludwig Wittgenstein (1953/1991) that holds that mental states are to

---

[22] For an overview of functionalist theories, see Levin (2018b).

be identified not with neural (or any other) physical states – or for that matter, with any sort of non-physical states – but rather with an individual's *dispositions to behave* in certain ways, under certain environmental conditions. For example, "*S* has a pain in her toe" is to be understood as "*S* is disposed (all things being equal) to wince, grimace, rub her toe, and ask for aspirin."

Philosophical Behaviorism, therefore, permits creatures of different physical types to be in the same mental states. In addition, according to its defenders, Philosophical Behaviorism can make sense of our conviction that (at least in many cases) we can know what others are thinking or feeling not by inferences on the order of "when I behave the way they do, I'm feeling a certain way, and therefore they must be feeling that way too" but just by looking (carefully). It can also explain how we can come to know what others are thinking or feeling even if we have never thought or felt that way ourselves. Yet another virtue is that it can explain why it is not hard to teach mental state vocabulary to young children: just as we can direct their attention to an apple and say "that's an apple," we can direct their attention to someone who is wincing and moaning and say "that person is in pain."

However, as many philosophers have argued, having these behavioral dispositions seems neither necessary nor sufficient for being in pain. To invoke Hilary Putnam's (1965) well-known example, one can coherently imagine a society (the "super-Spartans") whose inhabitants learn to suppress all pain behavior, including saying "yes" when asked whether something hurts – even when they are in agonizing pain and want it to stop – and thus, they can be in pain without being disposed to exhibit any pain behavior. Conversely, one can coherently imagine a society of "perfect actors," who are incapable of feeling pain but have become so skilled at exhibiting pain behavior (verbal and nonverbal) in the relevant circumstances that they become disposed to do so, even though they feel no pain at all.[23]

A better way to characterize the super-Spartans' mental state, Putnam argues, is as the disposition to exhibit pain behavior as long as one's desire to do so is not outweighed by the stronger desire to be stoic, and a better way to characterize the perfect actors' mental state is as the disposition to exhibit pain behavior as the result of the desire to deceive (or fit in, or get sympathy, etc.) and the belief that doing this is beneficial. In general, mental states are best defined not as dispositions to behave in certain ways given certain environmental stimulations but as dispositions to *interact with one another* as well as with environmental stimulations to produce behavior of various sorts, and individuals are

---

[23] See also Chisholm (1957) and Geach (1957) for similar objections to philosophical behaviorism, and Chomsky (1959) for an objection to the scientific behaviorism advanced by, among others, B.F. Skinner (1953).

best characterized as having mental states just in case they have (lower-order) internal states that interact in just those ways. This is just the sort of characterization of mental states that Role Functionalism provides.

Role Functionalism, therefore, is more inclusive than the Type Identity Theory and provides more resources for individuating mental states than Philosophical Behaviorism while preserving its distinctive view that mental states should be characterized not in terms of their internal composition, but their systematic role in producing behavior under a variety of conditions. But Role Functionalism invites a number of other questions, among them:

(1) What is the relation between Role Functionalism and Physicalism? At the end of Section 3, Role Functionalism was presented as a more inclusive alternative to the Type Identity Theory that Physicalists can embrace. However, nothing in the specification of this theory rules out the possibility that the states that occupy the relevant roles are nonphysical; after all, causal-relational descriptions are topic-neutral. So why should Physicalists embrace this view?

(2) Can higher-level role properties be genuine causes of behavior, or is the real causal work being done by the physical states that realize these roles?

(3) Can a "commonsense" or "folk" theory of mind of the sort that Lewis proposes make all the relevant distinctions among the different types of mental states that we recognize in experience, and if not, are there alternatives that can do better?

These questions will be addressed in order.

Strictly speaking, Role Functionalism is not a variety of Physicalism. According to Role Functionalism, to be in a mental state is not to have any particular *physical* property, but rather to have the higher-order property of possessing internal states that occupy certain causal roles, and as already noted, nothing in the specification of this theory rules out the possibility that the states that occupy those roles are nonphysical. However, although the causal role properties with which mental states are identified are not themselves physical properties, they do not introduce any nonphysical items or properties into the world. Thus, if they are realized by lower-order physical properties, there can be individuals with mental states in a purely physical world.

Moreover, insofar as it is unlikely (if not impossible) that nonphysical states could cause behavior and be caused by environmental stimulations, it is unlikely that there could be creatures with nonphysical states that play the same causal roles as our neural states. If this is so, then Role Functionalism would be a version of *Nonreductive Physicalism*, in which each particular instance (or token) of a mental state is identical with an instance (or token) of some physical state or other, even though these instances are not tokens of the same physical type. And since what makes each of these tokens a token of the same *mental* state is that they share a further higher-order topic-neutral property, this view is friendly to Physicalism, if not technically a variety of it.[24]

Many argue, however, that Physicalism demands more: it is not enough that as it happens, the pain role is occupied by C-fiber stimulations in us and by other types of physical states in Martians, androids, and so on. This leaves open the possibility that states with different functional roles – for example, feeling pleasure or having an afterimage of yellow-orange – could also be occupied by C-fiber stimulations, and thus, the tie between the mental and the physical would not be sufficiently tight. What is needed in addition is for the mental to *supervene* on the physical, that is, for there to be no mental differences without physical differences in the relevant domain. Returning to *pain*, if Physicalism requires that the mental supervene on the physical, then not only should the "pain role" be occupied only by physical states (e.g. C-fiber stimulations in us and other types of physical states in Martians and androids), but also all instances of those physical states that occur in the relevant population must be instances of pain.[25]

If mental state M supervenes on physical state P, then although (in contrast to the Type Identity Theory) being in mental state M does not necessitate being in physical state P, being in P necessitates being in M. And if, in addition, all states that occupy the causal-relational roles of our mental states are physical, then it seems that Role Functionalism is as friendly to Physicalism as any theory, short of the Type Identity Theory, could be.

Nonetheless, there is another challenge for Role Functionalism that is not faced by the Type Identity Theory, namely, the problem of mental causation.

The problem of mental causation is the worry that Role Functionalism cannot account for the causal efficacy of mental states. To focus once again on pain, it seems that if I put my hand near a hot stove, some physical disturbance in my hand will cause me to feel pain, which will, in turn, cause me to say "ouch" and pull my hand away from the burner. It seems, that is, that my feeling pain has a crucial role in explaining my behavior: If I hadn't felt pain, then why would

---

[24] Another influential version of Nonreductive Physicalism (Pereboom, 2011) denies even the Token Identity Thesis, and holds instead that tokens of mental properties are "constituted by" tokens of physical properties, in that each token of a mental property spatiotemporally coincides with a token of some physical property, and the instantiation of the physical property necessitates the instantiation of the mental property – but not vice versa.

[25] There remain questions, however, about whether physicalism (even with respect to mental states) requires merely "global" supervenience – that is, that there be no mental difference without a physical difference somewhere in the world – or "local" supervenience –that is, that there is no mental difference without a difference in the physical properties of some particular type of brain state.

I have pulled away my hand or said "ouch"? However, if every physical event has a complete, sufficient physical cause – as is now generally believed – then my saying "ouch" and pulling my hand away must be caused by the physical, presumably neural, state that realizes pain in me. But then, it seems, it is the lower-level neural state that is doing all the causal work, and my being in pain, if this is identified with being in a higher-order functional state, is causally irrelevant. This is known as the Causal Exclusion Argument, introduced and forcefully defended by Jaegwon Kim (1998), and many regard it as just as much a problem for Role Functionalism as for Property Dualism (as discussed in Section 2).

Many Role Functionalists, in response, argue that this worry arises from an overly mechanistic picture of causation, namely, that a genuine cause must "generate" or "produce" its effect, where this involves, if not actual contact (as suggested by Princess Elisabeth, when she posed a similar question to Descartes), then some sort of transfer of energy from cause to effect. However, they continue, this is not the only way to think about causation. Instead, causation could be regarded as a special sort of regularity that holds between cause and effect[26] or, alternatively, as a special sort of counterfactual dependence that holds between effects and their causes, on the order – very roughly – of "If the cause had not occurred, then the effect would not have occurred."[27] If either suggestion is correct, then functional role properties and the physical events or states that realize them could *both* count as causally efficacious.

Kim (along with others) responds to this suggestion by noting that if the functional states and the lower-level physical states that realize them both cause the behavior, then the cause of that behavior is *overdetermined* and argues that this leads to a number of problems. First, these cases are unlike the classic cases of overdetermination that we encounter in everyday life, such as two simultaneously thrown rocks that hit a window at the same time, each with enough force to break it, or the bullets shot simultaneously by two members of a firing squad that each hit the victim with lethal force. Second, these familiar cases of overdetermination are rare, whereas functional role-physical state causation would be ubiquitous, occurring every time a mental state causes behavior, and therefore, overdetermination provides an inadequate model of what is going on when my pain causes me to pull my hand away from the hot burner.

One response to this worry (developed in different ways by Yablo 1992 and Bennett 2007) is to argue that the causation of behavior by a lower-level neural

---

[26] See Melnyk (2003).

[27] See Loewer (2002) for an early example and Noordhof (2020) for a book-length development, of a counterfactual theory of causation.

state and a functional role state is ubiquitous because lower-level neural states *metaphysically necessitate* the functional states they realize. That is, if N is a realization of R, then necessarily, if S were to be in state N, then S would be in state R.[28] If this is so, there is an explanation for the ubiquity of the production of behavior by both mental and physical causes. This response is available to Role Functionalists and other Nonreductive Physicalists who maintain that mental states are not identical with, but are metaphysically necessitated by, physical states of various types. But this response is not available to Property Dualists, who (usually) maintain that there is no metaphysical necessitation of the mental by the physical; being in a physical state is neither necessary nor sufficient for having a thought, a desire, or a pain.[29] Nonetheless, this response remains controversial – and thus, whether mental causation provides an insurmountable problem for Role Functionalism (or any physicalistic theory other than the Type Identity theory) remains a matter of debate.

However, even if Role Functionalism can avoid the causal exclusion problem, there is another serious challenge to the view, namely, whether a theory of this sort has sufficient resources to make all the distinctions among types of mental states that we observe in ourselves (or have reason to believe could occur in others). This worry becomes particularly salient when we think about the commonsense theory of mind, associated with David Lewis, that has been the focus for the discussion of Role Functionalism so far.

Recall that our commonsense theory of mind (sometimes called "Analytic Functionalism" or "Folk Psychology") was introduced as a (simplistic) fragment of the collection of our shared "platitudes" about the causal roles and other topic-neutral relations among mental states, environmental stimulations, and behavior. The question now is whether any theory of this sort has the resources to make all the distinctions among mental states that we recognize from our experience. It may seem obvious that they don't; after all, aren't there mental states whose causes and effects we commonly know nothing about – and aren't there some "platitudes" about the interrelations among mental states that we just get wrong? In addition, it seems that the commonsense theory is particularly vulnerable to counterexamples. Consider, for example, that fragment of commonsense theory, discussed earlier, that focuses on pain, namely:

> *Pain* is the state that tends to be caused by bodily injury, to produce the belief that something is wrong with the body and the desire to be out of that state, to

---

[28] See also Antony and Levine (1997).

[29] However, if Nonreductive Physicalisms maintain that the relation between physical and mental states is merely *nomological* necessitation, then certain versions of Property Dualism are no worse off than Nonreductive Physicalism.

produce anxiety, and, in the absence of any stronger, conflicting desires, to cause wincing or moaning.

Causal-relational roles as simple as these, it may seem, can be occupied by systems that lack mentality altogether, for example, the economy of Bolivia or a homunculus-headed robot consisting of a billion individuals communicating with one another via cellphones with the goal of prompting a robot body to move in various trajectories around its environment (see Block 1980).

However, commonsense Functionalism has more resources than it may initially seem. First, the information it affords (at least arguably) need not be restricted to the "platitudes" that we can access immediately; it may take a certain amount of Socratic questioning to prompt us to recognize certain similarities and differences among the causal-relational properties of our mental states. The information accessed by this method, however, was always available to us at least in principle and so can count as the deliverances of common sense, rather than empirical investigation. Second, we can (and Lewis does) think of our commonsense theory as an *approximation* that gets things mostly right. Third, and perhaps most important, our common sense platitudes can, over time, be significantly modified by empirical theories while nonetheless retaining their status as commonsense platitudes, or close enough. (Not that this is always a good thing: think, for example, of how Freudian theory and various now discredited theories about the causes of autism, depression, and impulsive behavior once seemed to be the deliverances of common sense.)

There is another species of Role Functionalism, however, called *Empirical Functionalism* or *Psychofunctionalism*, that permits information from empirical psychology, cognitive science, and psychophysiology to be included in the specification of the causal-relational roles of mental states, no matter how far it departs from the deliverances of common sense. Psychofunctional theories can provide more detailed characterizations of mental states that could individuate them more finely than our commonsense theories and make them less likely to be realized by systems, such as the economy of Bolivia, that (at least seem to) have no mental states at all.

Nonetheless, there is a common problem faced by the Type Identity Theory and any version of Psychofunctionalism that diverges too far from our commonsense theory of mind. Given that psychofunctional characterizations of mental states are exclusively causal-relational, they – just like the characterizations of the commonsense theory – are topic-neutral. However, unlike commonsense characterizations, they do not purport to provide *translations*, or anything close to a priori equivalents, of our mental state terms or concepts. Thus, mental-psychofunctional identity statements, just like sensation-brain process identity statements, are subject to the "Distinct Property Objection," introduced in Section 3, and also a wide variety of arguments that have the same structure, and the same intuitive force, as Descartes's sixth Meditation argument for the distinction between mind and body.

The best-known contemporary arguments of this sort are the Modal Argument (Kripke 1980), the Zombie Argument (Chalmers 1996), the Bat Argument (Nagel 1974), and the Knowledge Argument (Jackson 1982).[30] These arguments are addressed in the following section.

5 Does Consciousness Have a Place in Nature?

As noted in Section 3, there is more to be said about the questions raised by the Distinct Property Objection to the Identity Thesis and the possible responses to those questions. In addition, similar questions arise from some more recent arguments against the Identity Thesis that can be extended to Psychofunctionalism. These arguments will be the focus here.

Most of these arguments are directed against Physicalist theories of mental states (such as bodily sensations and perceptual experiences) that have a characteristic "feel", states that there is *something that it is like* to be in. These are typically called "qualitative" or "phenomenal" states, and the properties that give them their distinctive feels (and provide challenges to Physicalism) are standardly called *qualia* (singular, *quale*). Whether these arguments can be extended to thoughts, beliefs, and other intentional states is a contentious question – and it will be addressed at the end of this section.

There are two broad categories of contemporary anti-Physicalist arguments: Conceivability Arguments and Knowledge Arguments. But although the premises of these arguments are different in interesting ways, they are ultimately supported by the same considerations.

One of the best-known Conceivability Arguments against the Identity Theory is the *Modal Argument* advanced by Saul Kripke (1980), namely:

1. I can imagine or conceive of a possible world in which pain exists in the absence of C-fiber stimulation (or vice versa).
2. If I can imagine or conceive of a possible world in which x exists in the absence of y (or vice versa), then there is a possible world in which x exists in the absence of y (or vice versa).
3. Therefore, there is a possible world in which pain exists in the absence of C-fiber stimulation (or vice versa).

---

[30] See Block (1980) and Searle (1980) for arguments similar to the Zombie Argument.

4. If there is a possible world in which pain exists in the absence of C-fiber stimulation (or vice versa), then "pain is C-fiber stimulation" is false.

THEREFORE
"Pain is C-fiber stimulation" is false.

This argument may seem familiar, and indeed, it should. As Kripke explicitly acknowledges, it is modeled on Descartes's sixth Meditation argument for mind–body distinctness (discussed in Section 2). There is a premise in this argument, however – premise 4 – that does not figure in the arguments against the identity thesis discussed so far, since it relies on a principle that the early Type Identity theorists did not explicitly endorse. They were concerned to establish only that statements such as "pain is C-fiber simulation," although not knowable a priori, could nonetheless be true. But premise 4 is based on the claim that if "pain is C-fiber simulation" is true, it must be *necessarily* true, true in *all possible* worlds in which the phenomena in question exist.[31]

This premise follows from Kripke's (then novel but now widely accepted) theory (1980) of how the references of "natural kind" terms such as "water," "lightning," "gold," and "heat" are determined, which has the consequence that these terms refer in all possible worlds to whatever they pick out in the actual world. Moreover, Kripke argues – and this too is widely, if not universally, accepted – sensation terms such as "pain" and "experience of a yellow-orange afterimage" can be viewed as natural kind terms, and therefore, their references are determined in the same way.

However, if this thesis is true and if, as seems hard to deny, scientific descriptions such as "H_2O," "mean kinetic energy" – and "C-fiber stimulation" – also denote at all possible worlds whatever they denote here in the actual world, then identity statements such as "water is H_2O" and also "pain is C-fiber stimulation" must, if true, be necessarily true – even if they are knowable only a posteriori. But then, if premises 1 and 2 of Kripke's Modal Argument are also true, the Identity Thesis is false.

It may seem, however, that premise 2 cannot be true. Suppose, as premise 1 maintains, that we can conceive or imagine being in pain without having anything specific (or anything at all) going on in our brains. But why, one may ask, is this significant: Can't we equally well conceive or imagine that scientific identity statements such as "water is H_2O" or "heat is mean kinetic energy" are false? For example, can't we conceive of a world in which we fill a pitcher with the liquid that comes out of the faucet, and later do a chemical

---

[31] Kripke presents his argument as a (perhaps unexpected) consequence of his then-innovative theory of reference.

analysis and discover that it is not composed of H_2O molecules, or a world in which we put our hand close to the fire, but instead of feeling heat we feel a chill or see a patch of blue? If so and if premise 2 is true as well, it would follow that water is not H_2O and heat is not mean kinetic energy. But we have reason to believe that these scientific statements are true, and therefore, that this premise must be false. In short, mental state–brain state identity statements are in the same boat as other scientific identities: if one gets rejected, so should they all.

Kripke argues, however, that this analogy fails. We may initially *think* we have conceived of a world in which there is water but not H_2O or a world in which there is mean kinetic energy but not heat, but upon further reflection – which includes reflection on our intuitions about reference and the essences of natural kinds, along with other background principles that we implicitly endorse – we will agree that we have *misdescribed* these worlds. What we are *really* conceiving of in the first situation, Kripke suggests, is not a world in which water exists in the absence of H_2O, but rather a world in which the stuff that comes out of the faucets, while colorless, odorless, and tasteless, is something other than H_2O. And what we are conceiving of in the second situation is not mean kinetic energy in the absence of heat, but rather a world in which mean kinetic energy exists but does not produce *sensations* of heat. Those are not worlds, however, in which there is genuine *water* without H_2O, but merely a water look-alike (and taste- and smell-alike), and these are not worlds in which there is mean kinetic energy but no genuine *heat* – but merely worlds in which heat does not feel the way it feels here.

In both cases, that is, we have described worlds containing items that lack certain *merely contingent* properties of heat or water, properties that they could exist without – or worlds in which there are items that possess those properties but are not heat or water. In these cases, we have conceived of worlds that are *qualitatively or epistemically similar* to worlds in which water exists in the absence of H_2O, or mean kinetic energy exists in the absence of heat, but are not the genuine article. Moreover, there is a similar explanation of what is going on when we think we have imagined a possible world in which other scientific identity statements are false (such as "lightning is a stream of photons" or "gold is Au").[32]

However, Kripke continues – and this is the crux of the argument – we cannot extend this explanation to identity statements linking mental and physical terms.

---

[32] And not only are these alternative descriptions of what we have conceived available, Kripke argues, but when we think seriously about the scenarios in question together with our other views about the world, we will prefer them to our original descriptions. (Yablo (1990/2009) calls this the 'psychoanalytic approach', since it requires thinkers to agree with the analysis after reflecting on their own states of mind.)

We cannot redescribe a world in which there seems to be a pain but no C-fiber stimulation as a world in which there is something that merely *feels like* pain – since any state that feels like pain *is* pain. Conversely, we cannot describe a world in which there seems to be C-fiber stimulation but not pain as a world in which C-fiber stimulation just doesn't feel painful, since any state that does not feel painful *is not* pain. That is, the only way we can specify a world in which there is pain – or not – is to specify a world that includes states *that feel a certain way* – or not – and *feeling that way* is an irreducibly qualitative property.[33]

This disparity is important if – as Kripke assumes – premise 2 of the Modal Argument is plausible, and therefore, the genuine conceivability of a world in which P is true is good evidence for its possibility. Given this assumption, the only way to prevent someone's claim to have conceived that P from entailing that P is possible is to argue that P is not genuinely conceivable after all.

It is clear, therefore, that not only is Kripke's argument similar to Descartes's argument in the sixth Meditation, but his responses to potential objections – and his implicit defense of premise 2 – have affinities with Descartes's responses to his critics as well. Just as Descartes counters Arnauld's claim to have conceived of a right triangle that does not satisfy the Pythagorean Theorem by saying (more or less), "If you really think about it, you will recognize you did no such thing," Kripke's (preemptive) response to those who claim that they can conceive of water in the absence of H_2O and so on is the same.[34]

As for premise 2, Kripke does not give any positive reason for endorsing this premise besides arguing, case by case, that there are no genuine counterexamples to it. Nonetheless, his attempt to sustain this premise has affinities with Descartes's attempt to show that clear and distinct understanding (if used correctly, of course) can reveal truths about the nature of things. To be sure, Kripke, unlike Descartes, does not invoke God's existence and nondeceptiveness to insure that there is a link between what we can (genuinely) conceive and what is possible. But we can understand them both as having the ultimate goal of establishing that it is possible to have knowledge about possibility and necessity

---

[33] Note the resemblance between this argument and the Distinct Property Objection. In both cases, there is alleged to be an important asymmetry that hinges on the inability of our mental state terms to pick out something in the world (or in possible worlds) without introducing an irreducibly mental property.

[34] This analogy is not exact, since "right triangles obey the Pythagorean theorem" is supposed to be knowable a priori, whereas "water is H_2O" is not. Some argue, however, that "water is H_2O" can be derived a priori from the statements that "water" is a natural kind term and that the essences of natural kinds flow from their microstructural compositions and that the microstructural composition of water is H_2O – but these statements themselves are controversial.

and that the only way to achieve it is through (the right sort of) intellectual reflection.

Another Conceivability Argument, directed more generally against all varieties of Physicalism, is David Chalmers's (1996) *Zombie Argument*, which begins by defining a *zombie* as a molecule for molecule duplicate of a conscious human being that has no conscious mental states; there is nothing that it's like to be a zombie. He then argues as follows:

(1) Zombies are conceivable.
(2) If zombies are conceivable, then zombies are metaphysically possible.
(3) If zombies are metaphysically possible, then Physicalism is false.

> THEREFORE
> Physicalism is false.

In this argument, just like the Modal Argument (and that of Descartes), premise (1) makes a claim about the conceivability of the physical as existing independently of anything mental, and premise (2) links the conceivability of this independent existence to its possibility. There are important differences between Kripke and Chalmers's defense of both premises,[35] but the basic lines of defense are similar: we can genuinely conceive of the existence of mental states in the absence of physical states (and vice versa), whereas we cannot genuinely conceive of the denials of other scientific identity statements – and genuine conceivability provides evidence for possibility.

The other important type of contemporary argument against Physicalism, the Knowledge Argument, begins with the claim that knowledge about the mental cannot be deduced from knowledge about the physical and concludes that the mental is something over and above the physical. Although the premises of the Knowledge Argument are superficially different from the premises of Conceivability Arguments, they are supported by the same considerations, and therefore, Physicalists can respond to both in similar ways. There are two versions of the Knowledge Argument that have prompted widespread discussion.

The first is Nagel's (1974) *Bat Argument*, which begins with the (reasonable) assumption that bats have conscious experiences – that is, that *there is*

---

[35] Instead of suggesting, like Kripke, that claims to have conceived a world that has water but not H_2O are mistaken, Chalmers distinguishes different types of conceivability (e.g. positive vs. negative and prima facie vs. ideal) and argues that only some of them provide evidence for possibility. In addition, Chalmers introduces a more general semantics (Two-Dimensional Semantics) that purports to explain why, in contrast to other scientific identity statements, there cannot be a possible world that is a mere qualitative stand-in for a world in which there is C-fiber stimulation without pain. See Chalmers (1996) for more details.

something that it is like to be a bat – but because of the systematic differences between bats' perceptual mechanisms and ours, their experiences of the world are radically different from our own. Nagel then argues:

(1) No matter how much we know about the physiology, behavior, and perceptual systems of bats, we cannot know what it is like to be a bat.
(2) If we cannot know what it is like to be a bat, then there is a fact about bat experience that is not a physical fact.
(3) If there is a fact about bat experience that is not a physical fact, then Physicalism is false.

THEREFORE
Physicalism is false.[36]

This argument has the same structure as Jackson's (1982) *Knowledge Argument*, in which he describes a brilliant neuroscientist, Mary, who has been born and raised in a black-and-white room but has nonetheless managed to learn all the physical and functional facts about human color experience via achromatic textbooks and videos. However, Jackson continues, it seems clear that if she were released from her room and presented with a ripe strawberry, she would be surprised by her experience and consider herself to have learned something new, namely, *what it is like* to see red. Jackson then argues as follows:

(1) Before leaving the black-and-white room, Mary knew all the physical-functional facts about the human color experience but did not know what it is like to see red.
(2) If someone can know all the physical-functional facts about the human color experience without knowing what it is like to see red, then there is a fact about the human color experience that is not a physical-functional fact.
(3) If there is a fact about human color experience that is not a physical-functional fact, then Physicalism is false.

THEREFORE
Physicalism is false.

Neither this argument nor Nagel's Bat Argument makes any explicit claim about what can be imagined or conceived or any explicit claim about the relation of the conceivability to possibility. However, both arguments have

---

[36] Nagel's conclusion isn't quite this strong, but rather that "physicalism is a position we cannot understand because we do not at present have any conception of how it might be true ... [and thus] an air of mysticism surrounds the identification" (1974).

important affinities with the Conceivability Arguments. First, they all claim that our conceptions of the mental and the physical are radically different: that there is an "explanatory" or "epistemic" gap between our theories of physical states and conscious mental states that does not occur between any other higher- and lower-level theories of the world.[37] Second, they all contend that this sort of epistemic gap entails a metaphysical gap: the radical independence of our conceptions of the mental and the physical entails (or at least provides good evidence) that these are conceptions of distinct types of things.

Many Physicalists have responded by challenging premise 1 in all these arguments and argue (following the tradition of Smart, Armstrong, and Lewis) that closer scrutiny will show that there is no epistemic gap between the physical and the mental. Others direct their objections to premise 2 and argue that even if there is an unbridgeable epistemic gap between the physical and the mental, it does not follow that that there is a metaphysical gap as well.

Chalmers (2002b) neatly taxonomizes the possible responses to these anti-Physicalist arguments: those who challenge premise 1 are Type A Physicalists, and those who challenge premise 2 are Type B Physicalists. In addition, there are Type C Physicalists who argue that the epistemic gap between the physical and the mental can be closed in principle, but that – for one reason or another – we do not possess the wherewithal to do so now.[38]

To challenge premise 1 of these arguments, Type A Physicalists argue that to genuinely conceive of the molecular duplicate of a conscious being, we must have in mind, and be able to attend to, all the details of its physical structure and functional organization. This is hard to achieve, but it is possible – and if we did succeed we would recognize that such creatures do indeed have conscious mental states. Similarly, Type A Physicalists argue that if Mary could internalize and concentrate sufficiently on all the knowledge about color experiences available to her in her black-and-white room, she would be able to know what it's like to have those experiences. There is, in short, an a priori link between our concepts of the mental and the physical (or functional) that we can now in principle discern, even though it may take effort to do so.

However, many theorists – both anti-Physicalist and Physicalist (e.g. Stoljar; 2001; Chalmers 2002b; Alter 2016) – remain skeptical and contend that physical and functional descriptions can provide information only about the "structure and dynamics" of what goes on in our brains and bodies. But these, they

---

[37] See Levine (1983), Chalmers (2002b), and Loar (1997). (The explanatory gap, Mary, zombies, Nagel's bat, and other characters from thought experiments about mental states have now earned a place in contemporary fiction: see David Lodge's (2001) novel, *Thinks.*)

[38] This characterization of Type C physicalism differs from Chalmers's (1996) earlier presentation of Type C physicalism as a variety of Property Dualism.

argue, are all *relational* properties, whereas the distinctive qualitative features of our experiences – the way they feel, or what it's like to have them – are *intrinsic* properties. Therefore, they continue, even exhaustive knowledge of, and attention to, the physical and functional facts would not yield knowledge of what it is like to see red or feel pain.

Some Type A Physicalists dispute the claim that these properties are intrinsic; after all, they ask, can we really conceive of a mental state as *pain* if it doesn't produce, among other things, a (nonderivative) desire for it to stop?[39] And can we really conceive of a mental state as an experience of red if we do not experience it as being similar to and different from other color experiences and prompting certain emotions? Anti-Physicalists will no doubt answer "yes, we can!" But even if Physicalists can make the case that playing a certain role in one's psychology is *necessary* for a mental state to be a pain, color experience, and so on, it is harder to argue that it is *sufficient*: it may seem that no matter how detailed and comprehensive our knowledge may be of the physical and functional states of another creature's brain and body, there is something about the qualitative character of their experiences that we still cannot know.

There are Type A Physicalists, however (most prominently Nemirow 1980; Lewis 1988), who acknowledge that knowing all the physical and functional facts about mental states does not guarantee knowledge of what it is like to have them. But this, they argue, does not threaten Physicalism: *knowing what it is like* to be in a mental state is not a species of factual knowledge, but rather a kind of know-how, or set of abilities; in particular, the abilities to *imagine, remember, or recognize* the states in question when presented with them again. This is known as the Ability Hypothesis, and it is often used to explain what Mary gains when she leaves her black-and-white room, if not knowledge of a fact about the experience that has eluded her so far.

The Ability Hypothesis can be viewed as a way to close the epistemic gap between the physical and the mental by reconstruing what this requires,[40] but many regard it as unconvincing: first, because there seem to be counterexamples to the identification of knowing what it's like with this particular set of abilities (see Conee 1994; Tye 2000), and more generally because it seems that what Mary lacks in the black-and-white room is not (just) a set of abilities of any sort but some *factual* knowledge about color experience.

---

[39] See Pallies (2021) for a recent discussion of this question.

[40] Indeed, Frank Jackson himself (2003, p. 439), in explaining his subsequent change of mind about the efficacy of the Knowledge Argument, remarks that as long as Mary's knowledge in her black-and-white room includes knowledge of what human color experiences *represent*, then "we have ended up agreeing with Laurence Nemirow and David Lewis on what happens to Mary on her release."

There is another possibility, however, for Physicalists whose goal is to challenge premise 1, namely, to embrace Type C Physicalism, the view that the epistemic gap between the physical and the mental can be closed in principle, but that we do not possess whatever it takes to do so now. The problem, as some Type C Physicalists argue, is that although we can construct a thought experiment in which Jackson's Mary has access to all the physical facts about color experiences, we ourselves do not now possess that knowledge. But if we did, they continue, we would be able to see how it entails facts about what it is like to have those experiences. This suggestion, however, is not widely accepted, since it seems implausible that the physical facts we do not yet know will be sufficiently different from the ones we do know now to make the connection between mental and physical facts intelligible.

A more plausible Type C suggestion, perhaps, is that we are now prevented from knowing what it is like to see red or be a bat because we lack the right concepts with which to characterize physical or mental states – concepts that would make the necessary connections between these states accessible a priori and, thereby, make it impossible to conceive of them as existing apart. Thomas Nagel proposes a number of ways to do this. One is to develop new concepts of conscious mental states that enable us to "think about the subjective character of experience ... [by means of] an objective phenomenology not dependent on empathy or the imagination" (Nagel 1974). Another is to develop new concepts of *both* our mental and physical states "[given that] our present conceptions of mind and body are radically inadequate to the reality, and do not provide us with adequate tools for *a priori* reasoning about them" (Nagel 1998, pp. 346–347). And in a later passage in the same paper, he suggests that what is required is "a third conception that does directly entail both the mental and the physical, and through which their necessary connection can become transparent to us" (Nagel 1998, p. 352).[41]

Accomplishing any of these conceptual transformations would be a difficult task, as Nagel acknowledges – but not impossible, at least in principle. On the other hand, Colin McGinn (1989) agrees that the mind–body problem cannot be solved without demonstrating an intelligible connection between the physical and the mental and that doing so is possible – but he argues that we humans are conceptually unsuited to the task. All we can do, McGinn concludes, is to reassure ourselves that although it may be impossible for *us* to know whether the mental extends beyond the physical, this knowledge is accessible to

---

[41] He has yet another suggestion, namely, "[w]e first have to interpret the third-person and first-person conditions of reference to mental states as inextricably connected in a single concept, but in a rather special way," in Nagel (2000, p. 448).

cognitive systems different from our own. This, however, is cold comfort for most Physicalists – and should be for anti-Physicalists as well.

Difficulties notwithstanding, some Physicalists retain hopes for a Type A (or Type C) response to the anti-Physicalist arguments – and indeed have offered new, potentially promising, approaches to the problem. But an increasing number endorse Type B responses to these arguments and deny that an epistemic gap between the physical and mental entails a metaphysical gap.

It is possible to deny premise 2 of the anti-Physicalist arguments by arguing that conceivability is *never* good evidence for possibility and that the scenarios depicted in thought experiments, particularly the outlandish ones such as zombies, Mary, or disembodied minds, are never reliable guides to modal facts (should there be any).[42] Most Type B Physicalists, however, accept conceivability as legitimate evidence for possibility in general but argue that it breaks down when what is being conceived is a physical system that lacks conscious experiences (or vice versa).

The reason for the breakdown, they argue, is that there are special sorts of concepts of mental states – call them *phenomenal concepts* – that are available only to those who have actually been in those mental states and acquired those concepts through introspection. These are new, first-personal concepts of one's mental states that have no connections whatsoever to any physical or functional concepts. Therefore, when we use them in thought experiments to consider whether individuals with certain physical characteristics must feel like this (pointing in) or whether individuals with experiences that feel like this must be physical, it is easy to see why the answer is "no," and perhaps even why, as McGinn puts it, mental–physical identity statements "strike . . . us as miraculous, eerie, even faintly comic" (1989, p. 349). However, the argument continues, these introspection-derived concepts do not provide access to any new facts about the experience but merely a new way of conceptualizing facts that we had access to before.

In short, the radical disconnect between phenomenal and physical (or functional) concepts explains why there is an epistemic gap between the physical and the phenomenal and why it will persist no matter how much additional knowledge we acquire of the physical and functional facts. It also explains why there is no reason to question the link between conceivability and possibility for anything other than the denials of phenomenal-physical identity statements, since they are the only ones composed of such radically disconnected concepts.

---

[42] This skepticism has a number of sources: naturalists' worries about a priori reasoning, experimental philosophers' worries that the intuitions prompted by these thought experiments are not sufficiently universal, and skepticism about the very existence of modal facts. Conversely, some physicalists argue that the epistemic gap occurs more widely. See Block and Stalnaker (1999).

However, this view raises an important – and familiar – question, namely, if phenomenal and physical concepts are so radically different, how could they be concepts of the same states? Wouldn't such identity statements be subject to the Distinct Property Objection?

Different Type B Physicalists address this objection in different ways, depending on their accounts of what phenomenal concepts are. One promising suggestion is that the phenomenal concepts of mental states acquired via introspection are *recognitional-demonstrative concepts* that get their reference in a distinctive way.[43]

For example, suppose that *S* is having a migraine for the first time, notices that unfamiliar experience, and thinks "what's *that*?" *S* has just acquired a new, first-personal concept of (an instance of) whichever internal state it was that came to *S*'s attention. Given that there are no logical restrictions on what demonstrative concepts can denote – they are perhaps the ultimate topic-neutral concepts – it is possible that this new, first-personal concept picks out an instance of one of *S*'s neural states, call it *N*. If, in addition, *S* is disposed to identify further instances of *N* as *that again*, or *another one of those* (e.g. "*that*, Madam, has not abated a bit!"), then *S* can have a new, first-personal concept of a *type* of neural state. Moreover, because these concepts, both type and token, are recognitional-demonstratives, they can pick out their referents *directly*, without needing to specify any distinct nonphysical properties of them.[44] Finally, if *that* (internal state) and *C-fiber stimulation* pick out the same type of internal state in all possible worlds and do so directly, then both can be regarded as revealing its essence – albeit in different ways.[45]

---

[43] See Loar (1997) for one of the earliest and best-developed versions of this view. See also Horgan (1984). For a different view of the nature of phenomenal concepts, see Papineau (2002) and Balog (2012).

[44] Can recognitional-demonstrative concepts – either type or token – pick out a determinate physical state directly, just by pointing? Levine (2010) argues not. He begins by arguing that someone who introduces a perceptual demonstrative to denote some property in the world (e.g. redness) cannot just point to a red object; they must selectively attend to its color, which requires an antecedent way of representing that object's color (as opposed to, say, its shape). Similarly, he argues, the successful introduction of a phenomenal recognitional-demonstrative concept requires some sort of selective attention to zero in on *which* property the concept is a concept of, and thereby requires some antecedent representation of that property. Levine notes a further indeterminacy that extends to phenomenal concepts: even if one attends only to the color (vs. shape) of a red object, it is indeterminate which color property is being demonstrated: is it scarlet, red, or even warm color? (See also Tye 2009, p. 45.) It seems, however, that a view like Loar's has an answer to both questions, namely, that the property in question (e.g. being an experience of red vs. square) and its degree of generality (e.g. being an experience of red vs. scarlet) can be determined by the subject's disposition to classify some, but not other, experiences as *another one of those*.

[45] Granted, this is a controversial view. See Goff (2017) for criticism and Diaz-Leon (2014) and Levin (2018a) for further explication and defense.

To be sure, as Type B Physicalists concede, these phenomenal-physical identity claims may continue to seem dubious, even if there is an explanation for why it seems that they may not, or even could not, be true. However, as some philosophers have argued, including Nagel himself (1965), this would not support Dualism, since if there were a developed theory of *immaterial* substances and properties that can be described objectively, then dualists would have to explain why being in a state that has the relevant immaterial property should *feel* a certain way.[46]

Nonetheless, there remain significant worries about Type B responses, among them, that if there were such a unique disconnect between physical and phenomenal concepts, the truth of physical–phenomenal identity statements would be uniquely inexplicable or "brute" and also that if phenomenal concepts work like demonstratives, it is hard to explain the rich knowledge we have of our own mental states.[47] Type B Physicalists have proposed answers to those questions, but they remain controversial – even among those who would be Physicalists.

In short, all these responses to the major anti-Physicalist arguments have difficulties and thus leave some unanswered questions about Physicalist theories of sensations and perceptual experiences. Until recently, however, there was at least some consensus that Physicalist theories of *intentional* states – such as thinking that it's time for lunch, wishing that it wasn't raining, and hoping that I didn't lose the keys to my car – are unthreatened by these arguments. The major challenge for such theories is to explain how mental states could be *about* something in the world outside the mind – and how a state's being about something in the world could play a role in explaining someone's behavior.

Now, however, many argue that (occurrent) thoughts, desires, and other intentional states pose the same problems for Physicalism as sensations and perceptual experiences because they too could not exist without having phenomenal character. Some argue, in addition, that any differences in one's intentional states – be they differences in what types of states they are or differences in what they are about – make for differences in their phenomenal character. And some go even further and argue that the phenomenal character of

---

[46] See Nagel (1965, p. 354):

> A non-corporeal substance seems safe only because in retreating from a physical substance as a candidate for the self, we are so much occupied with finding a subject whose states are ... mine ... that we simply postulate [one] without asking ourselves whether the same objections will not apply to it as well.

See also Frankish (2007) for an argument that a version of the Zombie Argument can be used to support physicalism.

[47] See Alter (2015); Goff (2017). See Levin (2007, 2018) and Diaz-Leon (2014) for an attempt to answer these questions.

intentional states is distinctive; what it's like to think that P has its own "cognitive phenomenology" that cannot be reduced to any sort of sensory imagery one may have when thinking this thought.[48]

If so, then all the questions just discussed about sensations and perceptual experiences will also arise for intentional states – and the Physicalists' responses will be equally effective or ineffective. Nonetheless, those other questions about the "aboutness" of intentional states pose special problems and need to be addressed as well. This will be the topic of the following section.

6 Intentional States

Consider the following mental states:

(1) S's belief that the meeting will be over by noon
(2) S's desire that the meeting will be over by noon
(3) S's fear that the meeting will be over by noon
(4) S's belief that it will rain tomorrow
(5) S's belief that the mail has come

States of this sort are often called *representational* states, for obvious reasons: they seem to represent, or be about, something outside themselves – and what they are about determines whether one's beliefs are true and one's desires, hopes, and fears are realized. They are also called *intentional* states, for historical reasons: the term, derived from the Latin *tendere*, meaning *to point*, was introduced by Franz Brentano (1874/2014), who was one of the first to focus attention on these states and their significance for theories of language and mind.[49] Among other things, Brentano observed that the special sort of about-ness possessed by intentional states has a number of distinctive features.[50]

For example, although we can infer, from "Howard ate all the filberts in the bowl," that there are no more filberts in the bowl, we cannot draw the same conclusion from "Howard *believes* that he ate all the filberts in the bowl"; he may think he had gotten them all but missed a few. And although we can infer "Howard ate all the hazelnuts in the bowl" from "Howard ate all the filberts in

---

[48] See Bayne and Montague (2011) for an overview of the strengths and weaknesses of these arguments.

[49] The form of these statements also explains why some philosophers call them "propositional attitudes", since the belief/hope/desire, etc. that P can be construed as different attitudes to the same proposition, and the hope that P and the hope that Q can be construed as the same attitude to different propositions – which can be true or false.

[50] Brentano, famously, characterized what intentional states are about – what it is that one believes, desires, hopes, intends, or fears – as having "intentional inexistence", but it remains controversial just what he meant by this locution. See Crane (2006) for a good overview. Also, see Chisholm (1957) for an influential account of Brentano's Thesis.

the bowl" and "Filberts are hazelnuts," we cannot infer "Howard believes that he ate all the hazelnuts in the bowl" from those same premises, since he may not realize that hazelnuts are filberts. And if we send him to the grocery store to get filberts, he may return empty-handed, even though there are (opaque) bags marked "hazelnuts" in plain sight. In addition, we can think about, desire, and hope for things that do not, or even could not, exist: for example, keys that never get lost, unicorns, eternal life, round squares.

Brentano argued that the special sort of aboutness possessed by these states is what distinguishes the mental from the physical; he called it the "mark of the mental." He also argued that it cannot be reduced to any sort of physical property or relation. This is known as *Brentano's Thesis*, and if true, it would pose a serious problem for Physicalism. It is important, therefore, for Physicalists to explain what it is for an intentional state to represent, or be about, something in this special way – and how to determine what, in particular, it is about – or to use a now-standard term for this phenomenon, what is its *representational content*.

There are many theories of intentionality, but they divide roughly into two groups: internalist theories, which characterize the representational content of S's intentional state solely in terms of properties intrinsic to S (at a time), and externalist theories, which characterize representational content in terms of the properties in the world to which S bears certain relations. On internalist theories, any two individuals intrinsically the same will have states with the same representational contents, whereas on externalist theories, different individuals can have states with different representational contents if there are differences in the worlds they inhabit, even though they are intrinsically the same.

One important internalist theory, articulated in the mid-1980s, is Conceptual Role Semantics (CRS), the view that the representational content of an intentional state can be identified with the role it plays in theoretical and practical reasoning.[51] Many regard CRS as a natural extension of the claim that the meaning of a linguistic expression is derived from the way it is used, and it has clear affinities with functionalist theories of the sort discussed in Section 4.

It is easy to see why CRS seems promising, since functionalist theories provide a plausible way to distinguish among different *types* of intentional states. Beliefs (roughly and among other things) are produced by perception, testimony, and inference from other beliefs; desires are produced by an individual's needs and by means-ends reasoning from other desires – and beliefs and desires interact in certain canonical ways to produce behavior. There are also

---

[51] See Block (1986) and Harman (1987), although Harman's considered view is partially externalist, in that he defines intentional states in terms of their typical effects not just on bodily movements but also on bodily movements that reach out to items in the individual's environment. See Field (1978) and Brandom (1994) for related views.

relevant functional differences between other types of intentional states, such as hopes, fears, and intentions.

In addition, it seems that differences in the representational contents of intentional states can be explicated as differences in their roles in theoretical and practical reasoning. For example, the contents of Howard's hazelnut-beliefs and his filbert-beliefs could be distinguished on the basis of differences in their effects on inference and their interactions with desires to produce behavior. In addition, beliefs about nonexistent things such as unicorns, eternal life – and keys that never get lost – could have representational contents if they have distinctive conceptual roles.

But CRS faces a number of objections. The first is whether it can permit different individuals to have intentional states with the same representational contents. After all, if the conceptual role of *S*'s intentional state is identified holistically with *all* its inferential and motivational relations to *S*'s other mental states, then it would be highly unlikely, if not impossible, for different individuals (or even the same individual at different times) to have states with the same representational content. It may be, for example, that both Howard's and Robert's belief that there are filberts in the bowl (given the desire to eat filberts) will prompt them to reach into the bowl. But if Howard's, but not Robert's, belief regularly prompts the thought of the sorry reign of Philibert Le Beau, then on this view, they cannot have the same representational contents.

This problem may seem easy to solve; all that is needed is to distinguish between those features of the conceptual role that contribute to a belief's meaning or content and those that are merely idiosyncratic. But there is no consensus about how, indeed whether, this can be done, especially given Quine's (1951) influential argument that there is no principled way to distinguish between claims that are true by virtue of meaning and those that are true as a matter of fact.

Moreover, even if there were a principled way to distinguish the idiosyncratic from the meaning-contributing features of a belief's conceptual role, CRS faces another challenge, namely, that certain differences in what, intuitively, an intentional state represents cannot be captured by *any* distinctions in the conceptual role. Consider indexical and demonstrative concepts such as *I, you, here, now, this,* and *that.* What *I* represent when I think "I am tired" seems as different from what *you* represent when you think "I am tired" as I am different from you, even if these thoughts play exactly the same role in our reasoning. And these cases are, at least arguably, merely the tip of the iceberg.

In a famous thought experiment directed against internalist theories of the meaning of natural kind terms, Hilary Putnam (1975) introduces Twin Earth, a planet just like Earth and all its inhabitants – except that the colorless odorless liquid that we (and they) call "water" is composed not of H_2O molecules, but instead the chemically different *XYZ*. Putnam then introduces an Earthling and Twin Earthling (equally ignorant of chemistry) whose water thoughts are prompted by perceptions and produce further beliefs, desires, and behavior in just the same way – and who each gaze at their respective oceans and say "the water looks cold." Putnam argues that in this situation, the Earthling and Twin Earthling mean something different when they say "water," despite their internal similarities – and that therefore, meaning "ain't in the head."

Many find this argument compelling and draw an analogous conclusion about the representational contents of their intentional states. In addition, Tyler Burge (1979) argues that this phenomenon extends beyond natural kind terms and concepts. In another well-known thought experiment, Burge introduces an individual *A* who has a limited amount of information, and a limited number of beliefs, about the syndrome we call "arthritis": *A* believes that he has arthritis in his wrists and knees, that he has had arthritis for years, that stiff joints are a symptom of arthritis, and that arthritis is painful. But *A* also believes that he has arthritis in his thigh – and this belief is false, since in our linguistic community, "arthritis" is correctly applied only to inflammation of the joints. Moreover, once *A* is told this, he defers to community usage and revises his usage to conform.

Burge then considers the possibility that *A* has exactly the same information and beliefs about the syndrome we call "arthritis" – but that contrary to fact, our linguistic community uses this term to denote ailments of the thigh as well as inflammation of the joints. If this had been so, Burge argues, "arthritis" would have correctly applied to *A*'s ailment, and *A*'s belief that he has arthritis in his thigh would have been *true* – even though what is "in *A*'s head," in both situations, would be exactly the same. Moreover, he argues, there are similarly compelling cases involving terms from many linguistic categories, for example, "brisket," "contract," "sofa," and "clavichord." If Burge is correct, then external factors play a substantial role in determining what intentional states are about.

Not everyone accepts these arguments.[52] But many who do suggest that we can have it both ways and that intentional states can possess two kinds of representational content: *narrow* and *wide*.[53] Narrow content, crucial for capturing the psychological similarities between ourselves and our counterparts, is determined by the intrinsic properties of the individuals in those states, whereas wide content, crucial for evaluating whether beliefs are true and desires are realized, is determined by the relation between those individuals and the items

---

[52] See Segal (2000).

[53] Dennett's term for narrow content is 'notional content', and Loar's is 'psychological content'.

that exist in whichever environments or linguistic communities they happen to be in. Moreover, some argue that there is no need to specify the meaning-relevant features of the conceptual role of an intentional state – or, for that matter, any of its intrinsic properties – to specify its narrow content: as Fodor (1987) puts it, there must be *some* intrinsic commonalities between ourselves and our Twin Earth (and other) counterparts, given that if we were in the same context, our concepts would pick out the same things.[54] Critics, however, object that even if there are such intrinsic commonalities, they would be too minimal and ineffable to provide an intuitively satisfying account of how our mental states represent the world *to us*, from *our* point of view.[55]

More recently, however, some philosophers have proposed a different, more substantive, way to think about narrow content, namely, that it derives from the special phenomenal "outer-directness" we experience when perceiving and thinking about the world. The outlines of this view, Phenomenal Intentionality, were suggested by Horgan and Tiensen (2002), Loar (2003), and Pitt (2004), and it has been developed into a full-fledged theory of representational content by (among others) Kriegel (2011) and Mendelovici (2018).

The guiding principle of this approach, as Horgan and Tiensen put it, is that "[t]here is a kind of intentionality, pervasive in human mental life, that is constitutively determined by phenomenology alone" (2002, p. 520). We encounter this phenomenal "outer-directness," a seemingly immediate presentation of items as outside our minds, most dramatically in perceptual experience, but many hold that it is present in thoughts, beliefs, and other (conscious) intentional states as well.[56] If this kind of intentionality is determined by phenomenology alone, then it is a good candidate for narrow content, since we can share it with our Twin Earth counterparts, disembodied brains in vats, and any other individuals phenomenologically like ourselves. Moreover, a view that derives representational content from the phenomenal character may be

---

[54] See Fodor (1987, p. 48) for the view depicted in the text, often called the 'mapping theory'. See also Lewis (1979), White (1982), Stalnaker (1999), Chalmers (2003) and Jackson (2003) for similar accounts of narrow content. Strictly speaking, these features would not by themselves determine whether an individual's beliefs are true and desires, etc. are satisfied; one would also have to specify the relevant context in which the belief or desire occurs.

[55] Indeed, because of these problems – and others – some philosophers question the need for anything like narrow content at all: why not understand the representational contents of individuals' intentional states to be determined by their systematic relations to items in their environments, and use, for a psychological explanation, whichever nonrepresentational similarities among these states best help to explain how mental states are produced by sensory perceptions and interact to produce behavior. See Fodor (1995, Lecture 2).

[56] Loar (2003/2015, p. 214) describes this feature of thoughts and experience as "the paint that points" and contends, moreover (p. 317), that "We are, it seems to me, as entitled to speak of phenomenal intentionality as we are of the felt qualities of a sensation."

better able than other theories of narrow content to specify just what those intrinsic properties are that psychological counterparts have in common.

Of course, Phenomenal Intentionality can provide a sufficiently comprehensive theory of narrow content only if there are phenomenal distinctions among our intentional states that reflect the intuitive distinctions that we make among them. This claim is contentious: Is there something distinctive that it is like to think that *P* for *every* instance of *P*? Even if it is true, however, Phenomenal Intentionalists need to say more about what it is to be in a state with the outer-directedness distinctive to phenomenal intentionality[57] and how the representational contents of simpler intentional states combine to yield contents of states that are more complex. Different versions of this approach propose different answers to these questions, and here too, the jury is out.[58]

In short, any "two-factor" account of representational content needs to specify more precisely what narrow content is supposed to be.[59] Moreover, both two factor and exclusively externalist theories face a further challenge, namely, to specify *which* relations between an individual and the world determine what that individual's state (widely) represents.

Many externalists begin by observing that meaning or representation seems to occur in nature: we say that the number of tree rings means (or represents) the age of a tree, that dark clouds mean rain, and that red spots mean measles. Thus, they suggest, an examination of how these "natural signs" work may help in developing a theory of mental representation that focuses on the relation between intentional states and the items in the environment that they represent.

In all these cases, the relation of signs to the conditions they represent is straightforward, namely, *reliable indication*; that is:

RI *X* represents *Y* if and only if:

(1) The presence (occurrence) of *X* is caused by the presence (occurrence) of *Y*.
(2) There is a law-like relation between the presence (occurrence) of *X* and the presence (occurrence) of *Y*.

RI, plus a caeteris paribus clause to rule out unusual occurrences, seems to capture the relation between natural signs and what they represent. However, RI cannot capture certain crucial features of the way that our intentional states

---

[57] See Bourget (2020), Mendelovici (2018), and Kriegel (20011) for competing views.

[58] Would embracing Phenomenal Intentionality support Brentano's Thesis? It may seem so at first glance. After all, as Horgan and Tienson (2002) argue, if Phenomenal Intentionality is required to give a full account of representational content, then theories of intentional states are no more immune to the hard problem of consciousness than theories of sensations and perceptual experiences. However, if Physicalists can show why the hard problem of consciousness is not a threat to Physicalism, then it may be easier to solve Brentano's Problem than it first appears.

[59] See Brown (2016) for a good overview of the topic.

represent the world. First, it cannot account for misrepresentation – and therefore for the possibility of false beliefs. If, on the basis of perception, we mistakenly believe that a small wolf is a dog or that an outbreak of eczema is measles, it seems reasonable to think that we're in states that represent what we perceived as, respectively, a dog and measles – and that therefore, we have *misrepresented* the things that caused those beliefs. But if representation is exclusively a matter of reliable indication, then given (a), our wolf- and eczema-caused beliefs can do no such thing. In addition, suppose that we always, as a matter of law, mistake small wolves for dogs when we see them at twilight. In this case, our dog beliefs would reliably indicate *either* dogs or small wolves seen at twilight – and therefore could not misrepresent those wolves as dogs.[60]

There are a number of ways that externalists try to augment or revise this definition: Dretske 1981) suggests that a state represents whatever it reliably indicates during an initial learning period; Fodor (1987) suggests that a state represents whatever it *asymmetrically depends* on: that is, if state A reliably indicates both Xs and Ys, then A can represent *X*s and not *Y*s if *A*'s reliably indicating *Y*s depends on *A*'s reliably indicating *X*s, but not vice versa.[61]

There are objections to all these views that have prompted further revisions and emendations, some more promising than others. But causal-informational theories have other difficulties as well. One, the Distality Problem, is to specify which of the many events in the causal chain that leads from an object in the world to the belief it produces is its genuine representational content. Why dogs rather than retinal stimulations, or something in between?

In addition, causal-informational theories owe an explanation of what it is for a belief (or hope or desire) to be about nonexistent items such as keys that never get lost, unicorns, or eternal life. In some cases, one could consider the representational content to be a composite of simpler properties that do exist, and this approach may work well for contents such as *keys that never get lost*. It is not clear, however, that it would work for beliefs that purport to represent natural kinds. For example, some argue that the representational content of a unicorn belief cannot be a composite of a *horse-like animal with a single horn in the middle of its forehead* (or any other combination of perceptible properties) since whether something would be a unicorn is a matter not of whether it has a certain cluster of properties, but of whether it possesses some "hidden essence." After all, a mutant animal with a single horn that has the DNA of a horse or an antelope would not, in our judgment, be a unicorn.

---

[60] This is known as the problem of disjunction.

[61] For example, A can represent dogs, but not small wolves seen at twilight, if A reliably indicates small wolves seen at twilight *because* A reliably indicates dogs, but not vice versa.

There is another way to revise RI that leads to a significantly different externalist approach to determining representational content. We legitimately consider a thermometer to be malfunctioning if it displays the same reading "n" for temperatures of n and higher, even if there is a lawlike connection between the thermometer's reading "n" and the ambient temperature's being n degrees or higher. This is because thermometers are artifacts designed to have a particular function, namely, to represent fine-grained differences in temperature (Dretske 1981).[62]

Human minds, of course, are not artifacts, and therefore, they are not (let us assume) the products of design. But they are (let us assume) the products of natural selection. Thus, as some philosophers argue, perhaps we can identify the representational contents of intentional states by examining their evolutionary function. This turn to evolutionary considerations shifts the focus from the environmental conditions that *cause* the occurrence of an intentional state to the *effects* that its occurrence, in the relevant environment, was selected to produce.

One influential version of this approach, known as *teleosemantics*, is due to Ruth Millikan (1984) and David Papineau (1987), who argue that an adequate theory of representational content must focus less on "production" than on "consumption"; less on what in the environment (reliably) causes an organism's intentional states; and more on the capacity of those states to produce behavior that is adaptive for the organisms in that environment.[63] This approach would help with the Distality Problem, since it is plausible to think that evolution selects for responses to macroscopic objects in an organism's environment rather than anything else in the causal chain that leads from those objects to belief.

In addition, the teleosemantic approach can accommodate cases in which a belief represents a particular type of object, even though the belief is caused more frequently by mere look-alikes. For example, even if saber-tooth tigers were few and far between in our ancestors' environment, compared to mere look-alikes, it makes intuitive sense to think of their flight responses as caused by saber tooth tiger beliefs, even if those beliefs often misrepresent a variety of other, less dangerous things. Better safe than sorry. In addition, teleosemantics can accommodate representations of at least some currently nonexistent objects – after all, saber-tooth tigers, once salient and dangerous, have long been gone from our environment, but our thoughts can still

---

[62] Conversely, he argues, we don't take paper clips to represent temperature, even though the volume of the metal varies lawfully with the temperature, because that is not what they're designed to do.

[63] See also Papineau (1987).

represent them. Nonetheless this theory, like indicator theories, has trouble with beliefs about unicorns and Santa Claus.

Yet another externalist theory, proposed by Karen Neander (2017), introduces features of indicator theories into teleosemantics to handle cases that pose problems for teleosemantics on its own. Even so, there remain problems for all externalist theories of content. One is what to say about *Swampman* (first introduced by Donald Davidson, 1987), a molecule for molecule duplicate of you that is created instantaneously when lightning hits a rock in a swamp. Given that this creature is exactly like you the moment it rises from the swamp, it may seem that it should have intentional states just like yours. But it has no causal-informational relations to anything in the world and no evolutionary history – so it can't.[64]

Externalists have tried to challenge the intuition that Swampman shares your intentional states, but this remains contentious. Yet another, perhaps more challenging, problem is whether any sort of causal theory can account for the representational contents of beliefs about abstract objects such as numbers or objects and kinds that do not yet exist (such as the neighbor's baby that is due next month or the novel species that the neighbor is creating in her lab).

However, while some philosophers (e.g. Neander) try to augment the causal relations between mind and world that determine the wide contents of an individual's intentional states, others offer a noncausal account that holds that the wide contents of intentional states are determined by finding an *isomorphism* between the narrow contents of intentional states and items in the world.[65] But this too is a controversial view. Yet others (e.g. Dennett 1981) suggest that the assignment of contents should instead be regarded instrumentally, as a matter of how best to *interpret* an individual's behavior, given their position in their environments and linguistic communities. Many philosophers, however, regard this view as dangerously close to eliminativism about intentional states.

In short, there remain problems both for internalist theories of content and the externalist theories just discussed. Nonetheless, Physicalists have made enough progress in developing theories of representational content to suggest that Brentano's Thesis, while still a formidable challenge to Physicalism, faces serious challenges itself.

---

[64] For those who object that Swampman is no serious counterexample to causal-informational theories, since its mental states would have the same causal-informational relations as yours to objects in the environment almost immediately after emerging from the swamp, consider instead a Swamp brain in a vat, which would have no causal-informational relations to anything.

[65] See Mendelovici's (2018) matching theory, which holds that ". . . a content matches another item when the item has all the features of the content's superficial character . . . [and that] . . . a content is true (or refers) if it matches some other item in the world."

What about Brentano's claim that intentionality is the mark of the mental: Are there genuinely mental states that do not possess it? As noted at the beginning of this section, there is growing consensus that at least some (conscious) intentional states, along with sensations and perceptual experiences, have phenomenal character and are therefore not immune to the arguments discussed in Section 5. There is also growing consensus among philosophers of mind that sensations and perceptual experiences have representational content: I look out of my window, and my perceptual experience represents the tree in my yard. I put my hand too close to the stove, and my pain represents some disturbance in my hand. Indeed, some philosophers argue that *all* phenomenal states have representational content, and if so, they too would possess the mark of the mental.[66] Granted, these states would not be immune to the worries about intentionality discussed here. But, by now, these worries should be familiar, if not easy to resolve.

There are other types of mental states that have not yet been considered, namely, emotions and moods. Emotions seem to have representational content: she's happy that she got the promotion; he's disappointed that they canceled the concert; I'm angry that you didn't wash the dishes. On the other hand, emotional states seem to have particular "feels" that are important to their identity: sadness, anger, and happiness. Are emotions best considered to be intentional or phenomenal (if it is possible to be exclusively one or the other)? And what about moods: Are they faint but long-lasting phenomenal states, or do they rather represent the world or the items in it as being (e.g.) rosy, hostile, or bleak? There is a lot of new work on these questions, and a range of theories have been presented about the nature of emotion and moods that span from purely qualitative to purely intentional – to a combination of the two that fit together in a variety of ways.[67] However, whatever the resolution of these questions, it is likely that any theory of emotions and moods will face both the hard problem of consciousness and Brentano's Problem. On the other hand, any responses to these problems that show promise for phenomenal and intentional states will show promise for emotions and moods as well.

Nonetheless, some philosophers remain pessimistic about the prospects for physicalistic theories of either intentional or phenomenal states – but also find serious problems with (any sort of) Dualism. They argue that the most promising account of the nature of conscious mental states may come from a different

---

[66] For arguments that all mental states are intentional, see Lycan (1987), Harman (1990), Tye (1992), and Byrne (2001). For arguments against this thesis, see Block (1998).

[67] See Pallies (2021) for a theory of emotions that combines the two and Kostochka (2021) for a novel theory of moods.

sort of theory altogether: Russellian Monism. This is the topic of the following section.

7 Russellian Monism

Dualism is the thesis that there are two (fundamental) types of things in the world, the mental and the physical, whereas Physicalism is the thesis that the only (fundamental) type of thing in the world is physical. Physicalism is thereby a species of Monism, the thesis that there is only one (fundamental) type of thing from which everything that exists derives. Another species of Monism is Idealism, the thesis that the only things in the world are mental entities, such as minds and mental states. Although many philosophers throughout its history have embraced Idealism as a theory of the fundamental nature of reality (or at least of the "real" world beyond the limits of human experience),[68] the major challenge for Idealism is to show how familiar everyday objects such as tables, houses, and rivers (as well as the elementary particles of physics) can be identified with or constructed from minds and mental states. These everyday objects, of course, include human bodies, but there is no particular difficulty for an idealistic account of bodies that does not also arise for tables, houses, and rivers. Thus a substantive evaluation of Idealism would go beyond the proper subject matter of the metaphysics of mind, and it will not be attempted here.

Nonetheless, there remain some questions about Idealism that *are* directly relevant to the metaphysics of mind, in particular, whether individual minds and their thoughts and sensations are basic constituents of the world, and if not, what the basic constituents are, and how they combine to produce conscious mental states that there is *something that it's like* to have. However, this is a question that arises as well for Panpsychism (discussed in Section 2), a version of Dualism that maintains that elementary particles possess both physical *and* mental properties, which can combine to produce macroscopic objects that have genuine conscious experiences. Thus, although specifying the "principles of combination" that describe how elements with mere glimmers of consciousness can combine to produce conscious beings with thoughts, perceptions, and sensations like our own is a difficult problem, if Panpsychism can solve it, this would resolve any "combination" questions that may arise for Idealism as well.

There is yet another species of monism that provides an alternative to both Physicalism and Idealism (and of course Dualism). This is Neutral Monism, the thesis that the fundamental elements of the world are *neither* mental *nor* physical, but rather a "neutral" set of properties that can be combined in one

---

[68] See, among others, Plato, Berkeley, Leibniz, Kant, Hegel, Bradley, Green, McTaggart, Cassirer, Royce, and more recently, Hofweber and Pearce.

way to produce physical objects such as houses, rivers, and trees (and of course the elementary particles of physics) – and in another way to produce mental states such as thoughts, sensations, and perceptual experiences. One perhaps familiar example is Hume's explanation of how a basic set of primitives – "perceptions of the mind" – could combine in one way to constitute enduring conscious minds and in another way to constitute phenomena in the external world.

Neutral Monism has had proponents throughout the history of philosophy, including Ernst Mach, William James, and Bertrand Russell – and, going back further, Hume and (at least arguably) Spinoza. Although Neutral Monism encompasses different views about what the principles of combination are, and even about what it is to be "neutral" and "monistic," the core idea is that minds and physical entities are composed of the same basic elements that are organized in different ways,[69] and therefore, like Physicalism and Idealism, it is simpler and more economical than Dualism.

Moreover, since macroscopic mental and physical properties are derived from the same neutral base, it seems no more mysterious that mental states can cause changes in states of the body than that states of the body can cause changes in other bodily states. However, unlike Physicalism and Idealism – which contend that the mental can be reduced to the physical, or vice versa – Neutral Monism does not give pride of place to either the mental or the physical and thereby avoids questions about how either of them could *really* be merely a species of the other. There remain questions, however – directed to many of these views – about whether the fundamental elements themselves are genuinely neutral or are better construed as either mental or physical; for example, are Hume's "perceptions of the mind" better regarded as exclusively mental?

There are other varieties of Neutral Monism that characterize the fundamental elements as abstract objects, for example, mathematical or geometrical phenomena, or perhaps even information. However, among contemporary philosophers, there is one variety of Neutral Monism that many find appealing not only for its simplicity but also for its potential to solve the mind–body problem, including the so-called hard problem of consciousness. This is Russellian Monism, named for Bertrand Russell, who introduced it in 1927, and it will be the focus of the rest of this section.[70]

---

[69] See Stubenberg (2018) for a comprehensive presentation of the varieties of Neutral Monism, their historical antecedents, their relative strengths and weaknesses, and the ways they are sometimes misunderstood.

[70] See Alter and Nagasawa (2015) for articles that provide many good accounts of the history of Russellian Monism and its strengths and weaknesses. See the chapter by Wishon for a good account of Russell's own views.

The argument for Russellian Monism begins with the premise that for something to be genuinely physical, it must be fully describable by the laws of the physical sciences. A second premise is that the laws of the physical sciences, down to the most elementary level, describe only the "structure and dynamics" of things in the world; only their dispositions to interact in certain ways under certain circumstances. However, the argument continues, the world cannot consist solely of dispositional properties; there must be intrinsic or categorical properties to ground those dispositions, to be the things that are so disposed.[71] But these categorical properties cannot be physical (since to be physical is to be fully describable by the physical laws) – and so there must be properties in the world that are not physical.

Not everyone accepts this argument. Some argue that dispositions can exist without being grounded in categorical properties; that it is perfectly coherent for our world to consist of "dispositions all the way down."[72] Others argue that both dispositional properties and the categorical properties that ground them can be physical if "physical" is understood in a broader, perhaps more intuitive, way.[73]

There are many philosophers, however, who are convinced by this argument – and go further to suggest that these categorical properties not only ground the laws of the physical sciences but also directly contribute to the phenomenal character of experiences such as feeling pain, having a yellow-orange afterimage, or seeing red. As Chalmers (2002a) points out, this feature of Russellian Monism makes it immune to the Zombie Argument. If our physical duplicates must be creatures that share not only our dispositional properties but also the categorical properties that ground them, then we cannot conceive of a physical duplicate of ourselves that is not conscious – because we cannot conceptualize those categorical properties in physical, or indeed any, discursive terms at all; they are "ineffable" or "inscrutable." And thus, the conceivability premise of the Zombie Argument – and all similar anti-Physicalist arguments – is false.

However, this argument raises questions about what we may be missing; what kind of properties are these categorical bases of the dispositional properties described by the physical sciences, and why would the ability to conceive of them – impossible though that may be – make it *unintelligible* that such a creature would lack conscious mental states like our own?

It is consistent with the distinction between categorical and dispositional properties that categorical properties serve as mere "thumbtacks": properties whose nature is exhausted by their role in grounding those dispositions. But for philosophers who believe that Russellian Monism can solve the hard problem of

---

[71] There is also a dispute about what it is for a property to be intrinsic. See Langton and Lewis (1998) and Pereboom (2011).

[72] See Bird (2007).   [73] See Stoljar (2001).

consciousness, the categorical properties that ground the physical dispositions must do more. As Chalmers puts it, the categorical grounds must not only be "distinct from structural properties [but there must be] an *a priori* entailment from truths about [them] (perhaps along with structural properties) to truths about the phenomenal properties that they constitute" (2013, p. 16). Similarly, as Goff, Seager, and Hermanson put it, the categorical properties must be "properties that in certain combinations *transparently account* for the existence of consciousness, in the sense that, if one could 'magically perceive' them, one could in principle move a priori from knowing the relevant facts about [these] properties to knowing the relevant facts about phenomenal properties" (2017, section 2.3). The question, therefore, is what sort of properties can do that.

One possibility is that these properties have at least some phenomenal character, which in certain combinations, but not in others, produces the full-fledged phenomenal properties such as what it is like to feel pain, have a yellow-orange afterimage, or see red that we encounter in our own experiences. This, of course, is a version of Panpsychism, and although it is embraced wholeheartedly by some contemporary philosophers (e.g. Strawson, 2015, discussed in Section 2), many resist the idea that elementary particles have any phenomenal character at all.

Alternatively, these categorical properties could be the proto-phenomenal properties discussed briefly in Section 2, properties that, although not themselves phenomenal, can nonetheless contribute to the phenomenal character of states such as feeling pain or seeing red. However, if these properties are the grounds of the dispositional properties described by physical sciences, then it is important to specify how they can produce experiences with phenomenal character if they themselves are merely potentially, but not actually, phenomenal. That is, Russellian Monists who suggest that the categorical properties are proto-phenomenal must be clear about what, if anything, distinguishes their view from panpsychism. This question remains the subject of active debate.[74]

Yet another possibility is that the categorical properties are physical but can in principle be conceptualized in a way that makes the connection between the physical and the phenomenal intelligible. These could be concepts that, as Thomas Nagel puts it, require "a third conception that does directly entail both the mental and the physical, and through which their necessary connection can become transparent to us" (1998, p. 352) or at least allow us "to interpret the third-person and first-person conditions of reference to mental states as inextricably connected in a single concept, but in a rather special way" (2000, p. 448).

---

[74] See Chalmers (2013).

However, if the categorical properties that can (perhaps) be conceptualized in this special way are themselves physical, then Russellian Monism looks to be a species of Physicalism. After all (as discussed in Section 5), Nagel's aim, when he speculates about the possibility of our developing these special concepts, is to show what it would take for us to be convinced that, and understand how, Physicalism could be true.

There are others who argue explicitly that the categorical properties could be physical: even if categorical properties have a substantive nature that makes them more than mere "thumbtacks" that ground physical dispositions, their existence is compatible with Physicalism as long as their role is not exclusively to contribute to the distinctive characteristics of conscious mental states; after all, proto-phenomenal properties are presumably protophysical too.[75] A view of this sort, however – if it does not require that we be able to conceptualize these properties in those special Nagelian ways – will not make the connection between physical and phenomenal properties "transparent," and therefore, Physicalists will have to revert to one or another of the traditional strategies to challenge the conceivability, modal, and knowledge arguments against Physicalism (see Section 5).

However, although there are challenges for explicating Russellian Monism and distinguishing it from both Dualism and Physicalism, many philosophers regard the distinction it makes between dispositional and categorical properties to be plausible and to open up new ways of thinking about the nature of the macroscopic physical properties in the world around us, as well as the nature of conscious mental states. It may be that further inquiry into the similarities and differences in how categorical properties contribute, respectively, to an individual's having dark hair and kicking a ball versus experiencing red and feeling pain will help make the connection between the categorical base and the phenomenal character of conscious mental states intelligible. Alternatively, it might diminish the intuition that there is a hard problem of consciousness at all.

All the metaphysical theories of mind examined in this volume have their strengths and weaknesses in accounting for the distinctive properties of phenomenal and intentional states. Most philosophers opt for one or the other (or sometimes a combination) and try to argue that the weaknesses are not devastating or that when properly considered, they turn out not to be weaknesses at all. However, there are some philosophers who believe that none of the theories examined so far can provide an adequate account of at least some species of mental states, and they therefore embrace Eliminativism, the view that those

---

[75] See Montero (2015) for an argument of this sort. See also Kind (2015) for an argument that Russellian Monism collapses into Physicalism or Dualism.

species of mental states, as least as we know them, do not exist. This view is the topic of the following section.

8 Eliminativism

Some philosophers find Dualism and Russellian Monism unacceptable and believe (or fear) that no version of Physicalism can provide a plausible account of the nature of mental states – and therefore deny that mental states, or at least certain types of mental states, exist. On this view, the attribution of beliefs, desires, sensations, and perceptual experiences to ourselves and others is merely a useful heuristic – if even that. This view is called Eliminativism (or Eliminative Materialism), and it has a variety of targets – and rationales.

Before proceeding, it is important to distinguish between elimination and reduction. To do this, consider the difference between the Type Identity Theory and the Token Identity Theory discussed in Section 3. According to the Type Identity Theory, each type of mental state is identical with some type of physical state; for example, *pain* is identical with *C-fiber stimulation*. This thesis has substantive empirical implications, among them that each instance of pain is an instance of C-fiber stimulation and that any (unmediated) effect of C-fiber stimulation on the body is an effect of pain on the body. In other domains, these correlations would support reduction, for example, from biological kinds (e.g. water and genes) to chemical kinds (e.g. H_2O and DNA). If determining the chemical composition of water and genes does not threaten their existence but instead reveals further facts about them, the same should be true for pain and C-fiber stimulation.

Granted, some correlations are insufficient for reduction. If we were to discover that the ghostly rasping that we hear in our car whenever we put on our seatbelts is produced by a rattle that is stuck under the driver's seat, we would not think that our ghost is identical with the rattle, but rather that there is no ghost. This, however, is because ghosts are antecedently defined as nonphysical things, and to say the same about pain would be to beg the question against Physicalism, since sensations, unlike ghosts, are not (or should not be) antecedently defined as nonphysical things.

On the other hand, suppose that only token identity is true; that each instance of a mental state is identical with an instance of some type of physical state or other, but not always with an instance of the same type. This thesis says nothing about mental *properties*, for example, *being a pain* – and there are two live possibilities. One is that there is a more abstract or relational property possessed by all instances of pain, for example, a certain functional role, and if so, then *being in pain* may be identified with, and thereby reduced to, that role. On the other hand, there may be no such abstract or relational property possessed by all instances of pain, and if so, then Physicalists would have to choose between accepting a dualist account of mental properties or denying that they exist, that is, embracing Eliminativism about mental properties (while retaining Physicalism for particular instances of mental states).

Even among Eliminativists, however, there are differences in the range of mental states whose existence is questioned, and differences in what precisely is being denied. Most philosophers direct their skepticism either to *qualia* or to the intentional states such as beliefs, desires, hopes, and fears that we attribute to ourselves and routinely invoke to explain and predict the behavior of others. And even those who advocate total elimination give different reasons for their skepticism about each type of mental state.

Qualia Eliminativists do not deny that we have conscious experiences such as being in pain or seeing red. What they deny is that the distinctive "feel" of a pain or an experience of red is due to its having a special sort of property – a *quale* – whose nature is revealed in introspection. They acknowledge that many are convinced that there are such special properties but attribute this conviction to some sort of mistake. They differ, however, about what the mistake is, and why it is so easy to make.

Dennett (1988) argues that we have pre-theoretic intuitions that qualia – the distinctive "feels" of our experiences – must be properties that are *ineffable* (unable to be described), *intrinsic, private,* and *directly or immediately apprehensible* in introspection. He then presents a number of engaging thought experiments designed to show that no mental state can have all these properties and thus that there are internal inconsistencies in the concept of qualia itself. He argues further that there is no obvious way to revise this concept to make it useful in our theorizing about the mind.[76] Therefore, he argues, the failure of Physicalism or Functionalism to accommodate qualia is to be expected, since there can be no such things (or, for that matter, anything close). However, even if conscious experiences have no *qualia*, as Dennett defines them, there is nonetheless something it is like to have them – or so it seems – and (as discussed in Sections 3 and 4) Physicalists must explain how these can exist in an exclusively physical world.

A more recent version of Qualia Eliminativism, due to Keith Frankish (2016), goes further and contends that conscious mental states have no special

---

[76] Georges Rey (1993), another qualia eliminativist, also denies that sensations and perceptions have properties over and above functional properties and attributes the widespread belief that they do to a kind of misinterpretation, influenced by Cartesian propaganda, of what goes on in introspection.

qualitative or phenomenal properties at all.[77] Frankish, like Dennett, suggests that the belief that there are such properties is based on a mistake, but he argues that the mistake is due to an introspective illusion that is just as mistaken as the belief, acquired while watching a skilled magician, that objects can be moved (directly) by the power of thought. (Indeed, this view has come to be known as "Illusionism.") We think, when we attend to a pain or an experience of red, that we have access to a special phenomenal property that makes it an experience of pain or of red. But what introspection really provides is access to physical properties that we *misrepresent* as phenomenal. Frankish calls these "quasi-phenomenal" properties and suggests, as an example, that "quasi-phenomenal redness is the physical property that typically triggers introspective representations of phenomenal redness" (2016, p.15).

Given this characterization of quasi-phenomenal properties, however, one may wonder why such a view counts as elimination rather than reduction. It may be, as Frankish suggests, that the quasi-phenomenal redness that triggers our introspective judgments is a "complex, gerrymandered" property. In this case, there would not even be a correlation between our introspective reports of phenomenal redness and a neurophysiological or psychofunctional property, and so it is plausible to think that reduction would fail. But if the property that standardly "triggers" these introspective reports is a neurophysiological or psychofunctional property, then why think that there are no qualia rather than that qualia are reducible to neurophysiological or psychofunctional properties?

Some Illusionists argue that in introspection, we represent quasi-phenomenal properties as being some sort of "perfect" or "simple" properties (e.g. perfect redness) that no physical state can possess.[78] If so, then taking these representations at face value would be just as problematic as attributing a ghostly rasp to the rattle under the seat that was making all that noise. So as go ghostly rasps, so go *qualia*. On the other hand, it is not clear that we need to think of introspection-derived concepts as representing quasi-phenomenal properties as simple or perfect, or for that matter, as representing them *as* anything at all. We may instead be picking them out directly by demonstration.[79] If so, then the lack of conceptual connection between those introspection-derived concepts and neurophysiological descriptions need not mean that they cannot denote the

---

[77] As Frankish puts it (2016, p. 14): "Illusionism makes a very strong claim: it claims that phenomenal consciousness is illusory; experiences do not really have qualitative, 'what-it's-like' properties, whether physical or non-physical. This should be distinguished from a weaker view according to which some of the supposed *features* of phenomenal consciousness are illusory."

[78] See Pereboom (2011, chapter 2).

[79] Granted, it remains a contentious question whether such direct demonstration is possible. See footnote 40 for further discussion.

same property, and thus elimination of qualia may not be needed to rescue Physicalism. This view of introspection-derived concepts, however, faces difficulties as well (see Section 5).

Qualia eliminativism is motivated primarily by the worry that if qualia exist, then Physicalism cannot be true. If as some have argued, intentional states such as having a thought or making a judgment also have phenomenal character – and have it essentially – then these worries (and potential responses) apply to them as well. However, there is independent motivation for eliminativism about intentional states that derives from a different source, namely, skepticism about the possibility of explaining human behavior as the product of beliefs, desires, and the other intentional states that figure in our commonsense theory of mind.

One of the best-known arguments for intentional eliminativism comes from Paul Churchland (1981), who argues that our commonsense (or Folk Psychological) theory of how intentional states explain behavior is "radically false."[80] The crux of Churchland's argument is that if we understand Folk Psychology to be an empirical theory, as we should, we will recognize that it has had "large-scale explanatory failures." Moreover, the only lower-level theory that *does* show promise as a systematic explanation of behavior is neurophysiology, and the generalizations of Folk Psychology do not map neatly, or even slightly messily, onto those. Thus, we cannot think of intentional states as being reducible to physical states that play a genuinely explanatory role – and should instead treat claims about what people believe, desire, and hope no more literally than claims that the sun rises in the east and sets in the west.[81]

However, although Churchland predicts that we will eventually become comfortable thinking of human behavior as produced by (e.g.) "a set or configuration of complex states, which are specified within the theory as figurative 'solids' within a four- or five -dimensional phase space" (1981, p. 84), others are skeptical. Indeed, as Lynne Rudder Baker puts it (1987, p. 134), speaking for many, to give up our commitment to the explanatory force and robust reality of intentional states would be to commit "cognitive suicide," or as Jerry Fodor puts it, speaking for at least some, "if commonsense intentional psychology really were to collapse, that would be, beyond comparison, the greatest intellectual catastrophe in the history of our species" (1987, p. xii). But Baker and Fodor argue – along with many others – that no such dire consequences loom.

---

[80] See also Churchland (1986).

[81] One may question whether explanatory failures of this sort show that intentional states do not exist. But Churchland assumes, correctly, that many Physicalists hold that the indispensable role of these states in explaining behavior is evidence that they are just as much a part of the world as chemical and biological kinds.

There are different ways, however, to defend Folk Psychology against Eliminativism. Some philosophers (e.g. Davidson 1970) argue that Folk Psychology should be treated as a normative theory that aims to depict what we should do, or would do if ideally rational, and not as any sort of empirical theory. Others (e.g. Dennett 1981) suggest that Folk Psychology can be sufficiently explanatory even if it does not mirror robust empirical generalizations as long as it provides a useful (perhaps practically essential) way to describe "patterns" in human behavior that will one day be more fully explained by a lower-level theory. Still others (e.g. Baker 1997) go further and argue that folk psychological generalizations support counterfactuals sufficiently well to permit intentional states to have genuine explanatory power and be "robustly real," even if they cannot be reduced to neurophysiological states.

There are also philosophers (e.g. Kitcher 1984; Horgan and Woodward 1985; Fodor 1987) who defend Folk Psychology as a straightforward empirical theory and challenge Churchland's argument on several counts. One is that many of what Churchland calls the explanatory failures of Folk Psychology are phenomena that Folk Psychology should not be expected to explain, even if they have something to do with minds and mental states.[82] These include, among other things, creative imagination, intelligence differences between individuals, the psychological function of sleep, and motor skills. They argue that if we treat Folk Psychology more narrowly, as attempting to provide (at least approximate) generalizations detailing how beliefs, desires, and other intentional states interact to produce behavior, then its prospects for being (at least approximately) explanatory may be better. They also contend that Folk Psychology is significantly less stagnant than Churchland suggests, and point to changes, over the years, in what we regard as commonsense explanations that derive from empirical discoveries.[83]

Moreover, they argue, the vindication of Folk Psychology as an empirical theory does not depend on its mapping smoothly onto neurophysiology, since there is a robust higher-level theory that explains behavior by appeal to computational relations among states with representational content, namely, cognitive psychology, which has made substantial progress since the middle of the twentieth century. Indeed, they argue, cognitive psychology is better able to capture generalizations about the causation of behavior than neurophysiological theories that begin from the bottom up. Thus, if the generalizations of Folk Psychology are approximations of at least a fragment of cognitive psychology, then it can be a genuinely explanatory theory.[84]

---

[82] After all, do we expect biology to explain the relative popularity of cat versus dog videos?

[83] See the discussion of commonsense Functionalism in Section 4.

[84] See Antony and Levine (1997).

Nonetheless, questions remain as to which features of Folk Psychology must be preserved for intentional explanation to be robustly real. In discussing Brentano's Problem and the attempts to solve it (in Section 6), it seemed plausible that no externalist theory could capture *all* our pre-theoretical intuitions as to which objects in the world a mental state represents. Similarly, there remain questions about the explanatory reach of internalist theories of narrow content and the relation of this content to items in the world. The question, therefore, is how many – and which – of these pre-theoretical intuitions about what represents what must be preserved for (commonsense) intentional explanation to be vindicated.

There are also questions about whether Folk Psychology provides the best account of the *types* of intentional states that explain human behavior. Consider the standard examples of commonsense intentional explanation that appeal to beliefs and desires:

(1) For any propositions *P* and *Q*: if *S* were to believe that *P*, and S were to believe that *P* entails *Q*, then *S* would believe that *Q*.

(2) For any propositions *P* and *Q*: if *S* were to desire that *Q* and if S were to believe that doing *P* is likely to bring about *Q* (and has no conflicting stronger desires), then *S* would do (or at least try to do) *P*.

Some philosophers argue that this picture is too simple to capture the nuances of what may be called "belief-discordant behavior." These are cases in which someone acts as if *P* were true but vehemently denies that *P* when asked – or vice versa. Well-known examples include the person who cannot bring herself to step onto the Grand Canyon Skywalk (a walkway over the Grand Canyon with transparent sides and floor) even though, after learning how well it performed on rigorous safety tests, she vehemently declares that it is absolutely safe, and the chocolate lover who watches fudge being made from pure ingredients and then shaped into pieces that look like dog feces and who then declares that there's nothing wrong with that fudge – but refuses to take a piece (Gendler 2008) or the (white) "implicit racist" who has studied all the literature addressing racial differences in intelligence and confidently declares that there are none – but nonetheless treats the in-class contribution of her white students more seriously than those from other ethnic groups (Schwitzgebel 2010). Do these people, in each case believe that *P* or not – and could there be a different answer for each case? It may be that a theory that can make these distinctions will force a revision in our commonsense views of what it is for someone to believe that *P*.

Another question is whether intentional explanations that appeal to beliefs, such as (1) and (2) provided previously, should appeal instead to an individual's degrees of confidence or credence. Do we get a more accurate explanation of *S*'s behavior if we specify that *S* is 90% versus 75% confident that *P*, or should there instead be some threshold for degrees of confidence that determines whether someone genuinely believes that *P*?[85] These questions too are contentious, but they point to yet another way that Folk Psychology may be open to revision.

But would this be revision – or elimination? As noted before, it seems that at least certain features of empirical psychological theories are absorbed into our commonsense intentional explanations, and therefore, one may wonder whether these new ways of thinking about beliefs and other intentional states would be candidates for absorption too. It is hard to say; the jury, once again, is out. But if, contrary to Churchland, Folk Psychology is less stagnant and more flexible than some philosophers believe – or fear – it may be easier than they think to preserve the robust reality of commonsense intentional explanation.

In short, there are some reasonable responses to arguments that purport to show that there are no mental states with the phenomenal or qualitative character that constitutes *what it is like to be in a mental state*, and there are some reasonable responses to arguments that purport to show that there are no mental states with representational contents. On the other hand, there are some further, more recently posed questions about the metaphysics of minds and mental states that challenge traditional assumptions made by both Dualists and Physicalists.

9 Some Further Questions

In a provocative paper, Andy Clark and David Chalmers ask the question: "Where does the mind stop and the world begin?" (1998). They make clear that they are not interested only in whether the *representational contents* of thoughts and beliefs must be determined by what is in the world, and not just "in the head" (as discussed in Section 6), but also in whether it makes sense to think that cognitive processes *themselves* could exist outside the head. Clark and Chalmers give a series of examples in which the use of external devices (such as smartphones) to store and retrieve information becomes so smoothly and routinely integrated into our interactions with the world that – or so they argue – it begins to seem unprincipled to maintain that these processes are essentially different from standard memory retrieval.[86] Since then, Clark has gone on to develop this Extended Mind Hypothesis further, suggesting that the simplest theories of humans' interactions with their environments may require

---

[85] See Frankish (2004) and Staffel (2019).

[86] Indeed, there is interesting work being done by neuroscientists and engineers to produce a prosthetic hippocampus outside the body that can receive and transmit neural signals for those with damage to their natural hippocampus. (See Berger et al. 2012). In these cases, it may be that the *brain* ain't in the head (or that the brain extends beyond the skin and skull)!

us to abandon the distinction between mind and world altogether and think of the units of explanation in radically different terms.[87]

This work, not surprisingly, is controversial; one common objection is that the functional similarity between standard and extended mental processes such as memory retrieval is less than the defenders of the Extended Mind Hypothesis suggest, and two common replies to this objection are that (1) increasingly sophisticated technology will diminish the functional differences between standard and extended mental processes and (2) the differences that remain are irrelevant. It is no doubt too early to evaluate this hypothesis with any sort of confidence.[88] Nonetheless, the questions it raises should be of interest not only to Physicalists and Role Functionalists but also to Dualists who hold that mental states are irreducibly mental properties of an individual's brain and body.

Another question of increasing interest to philosophers is whether groups of individuals, or entire communities, can possess mental states (e.g. beliefs, desires, intentions, and emotions) that cannot be reduced to the mental states of the individuals in those communities.[89] Is it merely metaphorical to say that a community (and not just the individuals in it) is pessimistic, or wants to succeed, or believes that intelligent beings from other planets live among us on Earth or remembers the 60s? Or can claims like this be literally true – and if so, how; does it matter how many members of the community in question individually possess the belief, intention, or emotion in question?[90] It is easy to see, moreover, that answers to these questions would have implications not only for theories of the metaphysics of mind but also for theories of what it takes to have self-knowledge and knowledge of other minds. They would also have implications for theories of moral evaluation: Desires and intentions lead to actions, and if a community intends to help resettle new immigrants or block access to a public beach, then whom (or what) can we legitimately praise and blame for

---

[87] See Manzotti (2017) for further argument that there is no genuine distinction between mind and world; this view requires a radical appraisal of what counts as the world, as well as what counts as a mind.

[88] See Adams and Aizawa (2009) and Rupert (2009) for a critique of this view. See Menary (2010) for a volume of articles that challenge and defend the view.. See also Gertler (2007) for a depiction of how our practices of attributing beliefs to individuals would change if the extended Mind Hypothesis were true.

[89] Some theories of "collective intentionality" identify the phenomenon as a special combination of other-regarding beliefs and intentions held by individuals in a community; see Sellars (1980), Searle (1990), and (arguably) Bratman (1993). The more radical view, emphasized in the text, is whether the communities as whole can possess beliefs, intentions, emotions, and other mental states.

[90] See, among others, Pettit (2009), Theiner, Allen, and Goldstone (2010), Gilbert (2013), Tuomela (2013), and Tollefson (2006) for arguments for the irreducibility of the mental states of groups to the mental states of the individuals in them and Rupert (2009) and Ludwig (2015) for arguments against. See Ludwig and Jankovic (2018) for a representative selection of both and Schweikard and Schmid (2020) for an overview of the subject.

these actions, and to whom (or what) do we have moral obligations? As with questions about the Extended Mind Hypothesis, these questions should have interest for Physicalists, Role Functionalists, and Dualists alike.

These questions, as noted, have just recently become the subjects of serious inquiry, and discussion of them has virtually just begun. Even now, however, it seems safe to predict that there will be new and interesting questions, and hypotheses, that need to be addressed by all the metaphysical theories of minds and mental states.

References

Adams, F. and Aizawa, K. (2009). "Why the Mind Is Still in the Head." In Philip Robbins and Murat Aydede (eds.), *The Cambridge Handbook of Situated Cognition*. New York: Cambridge University Press: 78–95.

Alter, T. (2016). "The Structure and Dynamics Argument against Materialism." *Noûs* 50(4): 794–815.

Alter, T. and Nagasawa, Y. (2015). *Consciousness in the Physical World: Perspectives on Russellian Monism*. New York: Oxford University Press.

Alter, T. and Walter, S. (2007). *Phenomenal Concepts and Phenomenal Knowledge*. New York: Oxford University Press.

Antony, L. and Levine, J. (1997). "Reduction with Autonomy." *Philosophical Perspectives* 11: 83–105.

Armstrong, D. (1981/2002). "The Causal Theory of the Mind." In Chalmers (2002a).

Arnauld, A. (1640). "Objections to Descartes's Meditations." In Bennett (2017).

Baker, L. R. (1987). *Saving Belief: A Critique of Physicalism*. Princeton, NJ: Princeton University Press.

Balog, K. (2012). "In Defense of the Phenomenal Concept Strategy." *Philosophy and Phenomenological Research* 84(1): 1–23.

Bayne, T. and Montague, M., eds. (2011). *Cognitive Phenomenology*. Oxford: Oxford University Press.

Bechtel, W. and Mundale, J. (1999). "Multiple Realizability Revisited: Linking Cognitive and Neural States." *Philosophy of Science* 66(2): 175–207.

Bennett, J. (2017). *Early Modern Texts*. www.earlymoderntexts.com/assets/pdfs/descartes1642.pdf

Bennett, K. (2007). "Mental Causation." *Philosophy Compass* 2: 316–337.

Berger, T. et al. (2012). "A Hippocampal Cognitive Prosthesis: Multi-Input, Multi-Output Nonlinear Modeling and VLSI Implementation." *IEEE Transactions on Neural Systems and Rehabilitation Engineering* 20(2): 198–211.

Bird, A. (2007). *Nature's Metaphysics: Laws and Properties*. Oxford: Oxford University Press.

Block, N. (1980). "Troubles with Functionalism." In Ned Block (ed.), *Readings in Philosophy of Psychology*, vol. 1. Cambridge, MA: Harvard University Press: 269–305.

Block, N. (1986). "Advertisement for a Semantics for Psychology." *Midwest Studies in Philosophy* 10(1): 615–678.

Block, N. (1998). "Is Experiencing Just Representing?" *Philosophy and Phenomenological Research* 58(3): 663–670.

Block, N. (2007). "Max Black's Objection to Mind-Body Identity." In Alter and Walter (2007).

Block, N. and Stalnaker, R. (1999). "Conceptual Analysis, Dualism, and the Explanatory Gap." *Philosophical Review* 108: 1–46.

Bourget, D. (2020). "Relational vs Adverbial Conceptions of Phenomenal Intentionality." In Arthur Sullivan (ed.), *Sensations, Thoughts, Language: Essays in Honor of Brian Loar*. New York: Routledge: 137–166.

Brandom, R. (1994). *Making it Explicit*. Cambridge, MA: Harvard University Press.

Bratman, M. (1993). "Shared Intention." *Ethics* 104: 97–113.

Brentano, F. (1874/2014). Psychology From an Empirical Standpoint. Routledge Classics. Oxfordshire: Routledge Press.

Brown, C. (2016). "Narrow Mental Content." In Edward N. Zalta (ed.), *The Stanford Encyclopedia of Philosophy*. https://plato.stanford.edu/archives/sum2016/entries/content-narrow/

Brüntrup, G. and Jaskolla, L., eds. (2016). *Panpsychism*. Oxford: Oxford University Press.

Burge, T. (1979). "Individualism and the Mental." *Midwest Studies in Philosophy* 4(1): 73–121.

Byrne, A. (2001). "Intentionalism Defended." *Philosophical Review* 110: 199–240.

Chalmers, D. J. (1995). "Facing Up to the Problem of Consciousness." *Journal of Consciousness Studies* 2: 200–219.

Chalmers, D. J. (1996). *The Conscious Mind*. New York: Oxford University Press.

Chalmers, D. J. (2002a). *Philosophy of Mind: Classical and Contemporary Readings*. New York: Oxford University Press.

Chalmers, D. J. (2002b). "Consciousness and its Place in Nature." In Chalmers (2000a).

Chalmers, D. J. (2003). "The Nature of Narrow Content." *Philosophical Issues* 13: 46–66.

Chalmers, D. J. (2012). *Constructing the World*. Oxford: Oxford University Press.

Chalmers, D. J. (2013). "Panpsychism and Panprotopsychism." *The Amherst Lecture in Philosophy* 8: 1–35. www.amherstlecture.org/chalmers2013/

Chisholm, R. (1957). "Intentional Inexistence." In *Perceiving: A Philosophical Study*. Cornell University Press: 95.

Chomsky. N. (1959). "A Review of B. F. Skinner's Verbal Behavior." *Language* 35 (1): 26–58.

Churchland, P. M. (1981). "Eliminative Materialism and the Propositional Attitudes." *Journal of Philosophy* 78: 67–90.

Churchland, P. S. (1986). *Neurophilosophy: Toward a Unified Science of the Mind-Brain*. Cambridge, MA: MIT Press.

Clark, A. and Chalmers, D. (1998). "The Extended Mind." *Analysis* 58: 10–23.

Conee, E. (1994). "Phenomenal Knowledge." *The Australasian Journal of Philosophy* 72(2): 136–150.

Crane, T. (2006). "Brentano's Concept of Intentional Inexistence." In Mark Textor (ed.), *The Austrian Contribution to Analytic Philosophy*. London: Routledge: 1–20.

Crane, T. (2016). *The Mechanical Mind*, 3rd ed. Oxfordshire, England: Routledge.

Davidson, D. (1970). "Mental Events." In Lawrence Foster and Joe William Swanson (eds.), *Experience and Theory*. Oxford: Clarendon Press: 207–224.

Davidson, D. (1987). "Knowing One's Own Mind." *Proceedings and Addresses of the American Philosophical Association* 61: 441–458.

Dennett, D. C. (1981). "True Believers: The Intentional Strategy and Why it Works." In Anthony F. Heath (ed.), *Scientific Explanations*. Oxford: Oxford University Press: 150–167.

Dennett, D. C. (1988). "Quining Qualia." In Anthony Marcel and Edoardo Bisiach (eds.), *Consciousness in Contemporary Science*. Oxford: Oxford University Press: 42–77.

Descartes, R. (1637/1984). *Discourse on the Method*. In J. Cottingham, R. Stoothoff, and D. Murdoch (trans.), *The Philosophical Writings of Descartes, Vol. I* (1984). New York: Cambridge University Press:111–151.

Descartes, R. (1641/1984). *Meditations on First Philosophy*. In J. Cottingham, R. Stoothoff, and D. Murdoch (trans.), *The Philosophical Writings of Descartes, Vol. II* (1984). New York: Cambridge University Press: 3–62.

Descartes, R. (1641/1984). Author's Response to Fourth Set of Objections. In J. Cottingham, R. Stoothoff, and D. Murdoch (trans.), *The Philosophical Writings of Descartes, Vol. II* (1984). New York: Cambridge University Press: 154–178.

Descartes, R. (1641/1984). Author's Response to Fifth Set of Objections. In J. Cottingham, R. Stoothoff, and D. Murdoch (trans.), *The Philosophical*

Writings of Descartes, Vol. II (1984). New York: Cambridge University Press: 241–277.

Descartes, R. (1643/2017). Correspondence with Elisabeth of Bohemia.

Descartes, R. (1649/1984). *The Passions of the Soul*. In J. Cottingham, R. Stoothoff, and D. Murdoch (trans.), *The Philosophical Writings of Descartes, Vol. I* (1984). New York: Cambridge University Press.

Diaz-Leon, E. (2014). "Do a Posteriori Physicalists Get Our Phenomenal Concepts Wrong?" *Ratio* 27(1): 1–16.

Dretske, F. (1981). *Knowledge and the Flow of Information*. Cambridge, MA: MIT Press.

Elisabeth of Bohemia (1643). "Letter to Descartes."In Bennett (2017).

Feigl, F. (1958/2002). "The 'Mental' and the 'Physical'." In Chalmers, D. J. (ed.) (2002), *Philosophy of Mind: Classical and Contemporary Readings*. New York: Oxford University Press: 65–72.

Field, H. (1978). "Mental Representation." *Erkenntnis* 13(1): 9–61.

Fodor, J. (1987). *Psychosemantics*. Cambridge, MA: MIT Press.

Fodor, J. (1995). *The Elm and the Expert: Mentalese and its Semantics*. Cambridge, MA: MIT Press.

Frankish, K. (2004). *Mind and Supermind*. Cambridge: Cambridge University Press.

Frankish, K. (2007). "The Anti-Zombie Argument." *The Philosophical Quarterly* 57(229): 650–666.

Frankish, K. (2016). "Illusionism as a Theory of Consciousness." *Journal of Consciousness Studies* 23(11–12): 11–39.

Frege, G. (1892/1960). *On Sense and Reference*. In P. Geach and M. Black (ed.), *Translations from the Philosophical Writings of Gottlob Frege*. . Oxford: Basil Blackwell, 1960.

Gassendi, P. (1640). "Objections to Descartes's Meditations." In Bennett (2017).

Geach, P. (1957). *Mental Acts*. Oxfordshire, England: Routledge and Kegan Paul.

Gendler, T. (2008). "Alief and Belief." *The Journal of Philosophy* 105(10): 634–663.

Gertler, B. (2007). "Overextending the Mind." In Brie Gertler and Lawrence Shapiro (eds.), *Arguing about the Mind*. Oxfordshire Routledge: 192–206.

Gilbert, M. (2013). *Joint Commitment: How We Make the Social World*. New York: Oxford University Press.

Goff, P. (2017). *Consciousness and Fundamental Reality*. New York: Oxford University Press.

Goff, P., Seager, W., and Hermanson, S. (2017). "Panpsychism." Stanford Encyclopedia of Philosophy. https://plato.stanford.edu/entries/panpsych ism/#RussMoni

Harman, G. (1987). "(Nonsolopsistic) Conceptual Role Semantics." In Ernest LePore (ed.), *New Directions in Semantics*. London: Academic Press: 55–81.

Harman, G. (1990). "The Intrinsic Quality of Experience." In Tomberlin, J. (ed.), *Action Theory and Philosophy of Mind (Philosophical Perspectives, Vol. 4)*. Atascadero, CA: Ridgeview: 31–52.

Hart, W. G. (1988). *The Engines of the Soul*. Cambridge: Cambridge University Press.

Hempel, C. (1969). "Reduction: Ontological and Linguistic Facets." In S. Morgenbesser, et al. (eds.), *Essays in Honor of Ernest Nagel*. New York: St Martin's Press, pp. 179–199.

Hobbes, T. (1651/2014). *The Leviathan*. In N. Malcolm (ed.). Oxford: Oxford University Press.

Hoffman, P. (1986). "The Unity of Descartes's Man." *Philosophical Review* 96 (3): 339–370.

Horgan, T. (1984). "Jackson on Physical Information and Qualia." *The Philosophical Quarterly*, 34(135): 147–152.

Horgan, T. and Tienson, J. (2002). "The Intentionality of Phenomenology and the Phenomenology of Intentionality." In Chalmers, D. (ed.) (2002), *Philosophy of Mind: Classical and Contemporary Readings*. New York: Oxford University Press: 520–533.

Horgan T. and Woodward, J. (1985). "Folk Psychology is Here to Stay." *The Philosophical Review* 94(2): 197–226.

Huxley, T. (1875/2002) "On the Hypothesis that Animals are Automata and its History." In Chalmers, D. (ed.) (2002). *Philosophy of Mind: Classical and Contemporary Readings*. New York: Oxford University Press: 24–30.

Jackson, F. (1982). "Epiphenomenal Qualia." *Philosophical Quarterly* 32: 127–136.

Jackson, F. (2003). Narrow Content and Representation, or Twin Earth Revisited. *Proceedings and Addresses of the American Philosophical Association* 77: 55–70.

Kim, J. (1979). "Causality, Identity, and Supervenience in the Mind-Body Problem." *Midwest Studies in Philosophy* 4: 31–50.

Kim, J. (1998). *Mind in a Physical World*: An Essay on the Mind-Body Problem and Mental Causation. Cambridge, MA: MIT Press.

Kind, A. (2015). "Pessimism About Russellian Monism." In T. Alter and Nagasawa, Y. (ed.), *Consciousness in the Physical World*. New York: Oxford University Press: 401–421.

Kitcher, P. (1984). "In Defense of Intentional Psychology." *Journal of Philosophy* 81: 89–106.

Kostochka, T. (2021). "Why Moods Change: Their Appropriateness and Connection to Beliefs." *Synthese* 198 (12): 11399–11420.

Kriegel, U. (2011). *The Sources of Intentionality*. New York: Oxford University Press.

Kripke, S. (1980). *Naming and Necessity*. Cambridge, MA: Harvard University Press.

Langton, R. and Lewis, D. (1998). "Defining 'Intrinsic." *Philosophy and Phenomenological Research* 58(2): 333–345.

Latham, N. (2001). "Substance Physicalism." in Carl Gillett and Barry Loewer, (eds.), *Physicalism and its Discontents*. Cambridge: Cambridge University Press: 152–171.

Leibniz, G. W. (1714/1991). *The Monadology*. In Leibniz, GW. (2010, D. Garber, and R. ariew trans.) *Discourse on Metaphysics and other Essays*. Indianapolis, IN: Hackett Publishing.

Levin, J. (2007). "What is a Phenomenal Concept?" In Alter, T., and Walter, S. (eds.), *Phenomenal Concepts and Phenomenal Knowledge*. New York: Oxford University Press: 87–110.

Levin, J. (2008). "Taking Type B Materialism Seriously." *Mind and Language* 23(4) (September): 402–425.

Levin, J. (2018a). "Once More Unto the Breach." *Australasian Journal of Philosophy* 97(1): 57–71.

Levin, J. (2018b). "Functionalism." *The Stanford Encyclopedia of Philosophy* (Fall 2018 Edition), Edward N. Zalta (ed.), https://plato.stanford.edu/arch ives/fall2018/entries/functionalism/.

Levin, J. (2020). "'Phenomenal States' and the Scope of the Phenomenal Concepts Strategy." In Sullivan, A. (ed.), *Sensations, Thoughts, Language: Essays in Honor of Brian Loar*. New York: Routledge Press: 289–313.

Levine, J. (1983). "Materialism and Qualia: The Explanatory Gap." *Pacific Philosophical Quarterly* 64: 354–361.

Levine, J. (2010). "Demonstrative Thought." *Mind and Language* 25(2): 169–195.

Lewis, D. (1972). "Psychophysical and Theoretical Identifications." *Australasian Journal of Philosophy* 50: 249–258.

Lewis, D. (1979). "Attitudes de dicto and de se." *Philosophical Review* 88: 513–543.

Lewis. D. (1988/1999). "What Experience Teaches." In D. Lewis. (1999). *Papers in Metaphysics and Epistemology.* Cambridge: Cambridge University Press: 262–290.

Loar, B. (1997). "Phenomenal States: Second Version." In N. Block, O. Flannagan, and G. Guzeldier (eds.), *The Nature of Consciousness: Philosophical Debates.* Cambridgr, MA: MIT Press: 597–616.

Loar, B. (2003). "Phenomenal intentionality as the Basis for Mental Content." In M. Hahn and B. Ramberg (eds.), *Reflections and Replies: Essays on the Philosophy of Tyler Burge.* Cambridge, MA: MIT Press: 229–257.

Loewer, B. (2002). "Comments on Jaegwon Kim's *Mind and the Physical World.*" *Philosophy and Phenomenological Research* 65(3): 655–662.

Lodge, D. (2001). *Thinks.* New York: Penguin Press.

Ludwig, K. (2015). "Is Distributed Cognition Group Level Cognition?" *Journal of Social Ontology* 1(2): 189–224. De Gruyter.

Ludwig, K. and Jankovic, M. (2018). *The Routledge Handbook of Collective Intentionality.* Oxfordshire, England: Routledge Press.

Lycan, W. G. (1987). *Consciousness.* Cambridge, MA: Bradford Books / MIT Press.

Malcolm, N. (1968). "The Conceivability of Mechanism." *Philosophical Review* 77: 45–72.

Manzotti, R. (2017). *The Spread Mind: Why Consciousness and the World are One.* New York: O/R Books.

McGinn, C. (1989). "Can We Solve the Mind-Body Problem?." *Mind* 98: 349–366.

Melnyk, A. (2003). "Some Evidence for Physicalism." In Sven Walter and Heinz-Dieter Heckmann (eds.), *Physicalism and Mental Causation: The Metaphysics of Mind and Action.* Exeter, UK: Imprint Academic, 2003

Menary, R. (ed.), (2010). *The Extended Mind.* Cambridge, MA: MIT Press

Mendelovici, A. (2018). *The Phenomenal Basis of Intentionality.* New York: Oxford University Press.

Millikan, R. (1984). *Language, Thought and Other Biological Categories.* Cambridge, MA: MIT Press.

Montero, B. (2015). "Russellian Physicalism." In Alter, T. and Nagasawa, Y. (eds.) (2015). *Consciousness in the Physical World.* New York: Oxford University Press: 209–223..

Nagel, T. (1965). "Physicalism." *Philosophical Review* 64: 339–356.

Nagel, T. (1974). "What is it Like to Be a Bat?" *Philosophical Review* 83: 435–450.

Nagel, T. (1979). "Panpsychism." In Nagel, T. (ed.), *Mortal Questions.* New York: Cambridge University Press: 181–195.

Nagel, T. (1998). "Conceiving the Impossible and the Mind-Body Problem." *Philosophy* 73(285): 337–352

Nagel, T. (2000). 'The Psychophysical Nexus'. *New Essays on the A Priori.* Paul Boghossian and Christopher Peacocke (eds.), Oxford: Clarendon Press: 432–471.

Neander, K. (2017). *A Mark of the Mental.* Cambridge, MA: MIT Press.

Nemirow, L. (1980). "Review of Nagel, T. *Mortal Questions.*" *Philosophical Review* 89: 475–476.

Noordhof, P. (2020). *A Variety of Causes.* Oxford: Oxford University Press.

Pallies, D. (2021). "An Honest Look at Hybrid Theories of Pleasure." *Philosophical Studies* 178(3): 887–907.

Papineau, D. (1987). *Reality and Representation.* Oxford: Basil Blackwell.

Papineau, D. (2002). *Thinking About Consciousness.* Oxford: Oxford University Press.

Pereboom, D. (2011). *Consciousness and the Prospects of Physicalism.* New York: Oxford University Press.

Pitt, D. (2004). "The Phenomenology of Cognition Or What Is It Like to Think That P?" *Philosophy and Phenomenological Research* 69(1): 1–36.

Pettit, P. (2009). "The Reality of Group Agents." In C. Mantzavinos (ed.), *Philosophy of the Social Sciences: Philosophical Theory and Scientific Practice*, Cambridge: Cambridge University Press: 67–91.

Place, U. T. (1956/2002). "Is Consciousness a Brain Process?." In Chalmers, D. J. (ed.) (2002), *Philosophy of Mind: Classical and Contemporary Readings.* New York: Oxford University Press: 55–59.

Polger, T. and Shapiro, L. (2018). *The Multiple Realization Book.* Oxford: Oxford University Press.

Putnam, H. (1965). "Brains and Behavior." In R. Butler (ed.), *Analytical Philosophy, Second Series.* Oxford: Basil Blackwell: 1–19.

Putnam, H. (1975). "The Meaning of 'Meaning'." In K. Gunderson (ed.), *Language, Mind, and Knowledge.* Minneapolis, MN: University of Minnesota Press: 131–193.

Quine, W. V. O. (1951). "Two Dogmas of Empiricism." *The Philosophical Review* 60 (1951): 20–43.

Ryle, G. (1949). *The Concept of Mind.* Chicago: University of Chicago Press.

Rey, G. (1993). "Sensational Sentences." In Martin Davies and Glyn W. Humphreys (eds.), *Consciousness: Philosophical and Psychological Essays.* Oxford: Blackwell (1993)

Rupert, R. (2009). *Cognitive Systems and the Extended Mind.* New York: Oxford University Press.

Russell, B. (1927). *The Analysis of Matter.* London: Kegan Paul.

Schweikard, D. P. and Hans B. S. (2020). "Collective Intentionality." In Edward N. Zalta (ed.), *The Stanford Encyclopedia of Philosophy* (Winter 2020 Edition), https://plato.stanford.edu/archives/win2020/entries/collective-intentionality/.

Schwitzgebel, E. (2010). "Acting Contrary to our Professed Beliefs or the Gulf Between Occurrent Judgment and Disposiional Belief." *Pacific Philosophical Quarterly* Vol 91, Issue 4: 53–553.

Schwitzgebel, E. (2014). "The Crazyist Theory of Mind." *Australasian Journal of Philosophy* 92: 665–682.

Seager, W. ed. (2020). *The Routledge Handbook of Panpsychism*. New York. Routlaege Press.

Searle, J. (1980). "Minds, Brains, and Programs." *Behavioral and Brain Sciences* 3: 417–424.

Searle, J. (1990). "Collective Intentions and Actions." In P. Cohen, J. Morgan, and M. E. Pollack (eds.), *Intentions in Communication*. Cambridge, MA: Bradford Books, MIT Press: 401–415.

Segal, G. (2000). *A Slim Book about Narrow Content*. Cambridge, MA: MIT Press.

Sellars, W. (1980). "On Reasoning about Values." *American Philosophical Quarterly* 17(2): 81–101.

Skinner, B. F. (1953). *Science and Human Behavior*. New York: Macmillan.

Smart, J. J. C. (1959/2002). "Sensations and Brain Processes." In Chalmers, D. J. (ed.) (2002), *Philosophy of Mind: Classical and Contemporary Readings*. New York: Oxford University Press: 60–67.

Staffel, J. (2019). *Unsettled Thoughts*. New York: Oxford University Press.

Stalnaker, R. (1999). *Context and Content*. Oxford: Oxford University Press.

Stoljar, D. (2001). "Two Conceptions of the Physical." *Philosophy and Phenomenological Research* 62: 253–281.

Strawson, G. (2015). "Real Materialism (with new postscript)." In Alter, T. and Nagasawa, Y. (eds.) (2015), *Consciousness in the Physical World*. New York: Oxford University Press: 161–208.

Stubenberg, L. (2018). "Neutral Monism." In Edward N. Zalta (ed.), *The Stanford Encyclopedia of Philosophy* (Fall 2018 Edition), https://plato.stanford.edu/archives/fall2018/entries/neutral-monism/.

Theiner, G., C. Allen, and Goldstone R. L. (2010). "Recognizing Group Cognition." In *Cognitive Systems Research* 11(4): 378–395.

Tollefsen, D. (2006) "From Extended Mind to Collective Mind." *Cognitive Systems Research* 7: 140–150.

Tuomela, R. (2013). *Social Ontology: Collective Intentionality and Group Agents*. New York: Oxford University Press.

Tye, M. (1992). "Visual Qualia and Visual Content." in T. Crane (ed.), *The Contents of Experience*. Cambridge: Cambridge University Press.

Tye, M. (2000). *Consciousness, Color, and Content*. Cambridge, MA: MIT Press.

Tye, M. (2009). *Consciousness Revisited*. Cambridge, MA: MIT Press.

White, S. (1982). "Partial Character and the Language of Thought," *Pacific Philosophical Quarterly* 63: 347–365.

White, S. (2007). "Property Dualism, Phenomenal Concepts, and the Semantic Premise." In T. Alter and Walter, S. (eds.) (2007), *Phenomenal Concepts and Phenomenal Knowledge*. Oxford: Oxford University Press: 210–248.

Wishon, D. (2015). "Russell on Russellian Monism." In Alter, T. and Nagasawa, Y. (eds.) (2015). *Consciousness in the Physical World*. New York: Oxford University Press: 91–118.

Wittgenstein, L. (1953/1991). *The Philosophical Investigations*. In G.E. M. Anscombe (ed.). Hoboken. NJ: Wiley Blackwell Publishing.

Yablo, S. (1992). "Mental Causation." *Philosophical Review* 101: 245–280.

Yablo, S. (1990/2009). "No Fool's Cold: Notes on Illusions of Possibility." In Yablo, S. (ed.), *Thoughts*. New York: Oxford University Press: 151–170.

Yli-Vakkuri, J. and Hawthorne, J. (2018). *Narrow Content*. Oxford:, Oxford University Press

Cambridge Elements ≡

Philosophy of Mind

Keith Frankish
The University of Sheffield

Keith Frankish is a philosopher specializing in philosophy of mind, philosophy of psychology, and philosophy of cognitive science. He is the author of *Mind and Supermind* (2004) and *Consciousness* (2005) and has also edited or coedited several collections of essays, including *The Cambridge Handbook of Cognitive Science* (2012), *The Cambridge Handbook of Artificial Intelligence* (2014) (both with William Ramsey), and *Illusionism as a Theory of Consciousness* (2017).

About the Series

This series provides concise, authoritative introductions to contemporary work in philosophy of mind, written by leading researchers and including both established and emerging topics. It provides an entry point to the primary literature and will be the standard resource for researchers, students, and anyone wanting a firm grounding in this fascinating field.

Printed in the United States
by Baker & Taylor Publisher Services